THE GREAT AND TERRIBLE L

The Great and Terrible Day of the Lord

by

REV. C. S. McKELVEY

Edited and introduced by
DR. MICHAEL D. BENNETT

Published by
BIBLE TRUTH PUBLISHERS
LONDON
1979

All the people who say we are down and out and passing away like all the other empires before us, know nothing of the plans of the Lord. Over three thousand years ago the Lord formed Israel with the one objective, to glorify His Holy Name, and it is His sovereign will that we do so, in spite of our waywardness. So He will bring us back to Himself in our affliction, and we will obey Him willingly and proudly as His servant nation, inspired by the Holy Spirit.

C. S. McKelvey

First published June 1979

© 1979 Bible Truth Publishers
(c/o Delderfield Press Ltd., Exmouth)

ISBN 0 906755 01 8 paper
ISBN 0 906755 00 X cased
Printed in Great Britain by
Delderfield Press Ltd.,
Chapel Hill,
Exmouth, Devon

CONTENTS

		Page
Preface		vii
Introduction		ix
1.	Future Figures in Focus	1
2.	Satan and the Fourfold Defence of Israel	12
3.	The Boast of Babylon – Mother and Daughter	18
4.	The Rule of the Beast	26
5.	Economic Judgment on the Nations and the Mark of the Beast	35
6.	The Plagues (Part 1)	43
7.	The Plagues (Part 2)	51
8.	The False Prophet and Judgment on Levi and Judah	61
9.	The Division of the Nations	70
10.	Sights of the Future	79
11.	A study of Isaiah Chapter Forty-two	89
12.	Jacob's Trouble	98
13.	The Two Plans – God's and Satan's	107
14.	The Beast – Gog, King of the North	116
15.	The Two Armies – Angelic and Human	126
16.	The Coming of the Saints	133
17.	The Armies of the Lord	143
18.	Conditions just before the Lord's Return – seen from Jerusalem	154
19.	Last Acts of the Present Age	162
	Glossary	173
	Subject Index	181
	Scripture Index	187

PREFACE

ALL the articles, now presented as chapters in this book, were first published during the period January 1975 to August 1977 in the magazine *Bible Truth*, of which their author was co-editor. *Bible Truth* is the official magazine of 'The British Israel Bible Truth Fellowship' of which Rev. C. S. McKelvey was the Founder Organizer. Following his death in February 1976 his friends asked whether these articles could be republished in book form. It was in ready response to these requests that the Council of the British Israel Bible Truth Fellowship passed a resolution in November 1976, affirming their intention to undertake this venture, and encouraging those responsible to initiate and expedite the necessary work. For more than two years numerous difficulties inhibited the work, and at times it seemed impossible that the book would ever materialize. Now, with each article lightly edited as a separate chapter, and with the addition of a glossary and two indexes, this work is finally complete. It is, therefore, with great pleasure that we publish *'The Great and Terrible Day of the Lord'* as a memorial to our old friend Rev. C. S. McKelvey.

May it be to the glory of God and the edification of its readers.

The Council,
The British Israel
Bible Truth Fellowship,
London.
(Registered Charity No. 272447)
1979

INTRODUCTION

And he said unto me, My grace is sufficient for thee: for my strength is made perfect in weakness. Most gladly therefore will I rather glory in my infirmities, that the power of Christ may rest upon me. Therefore I take pleasure in infirmities, in reproaches, in necessities, in persecutions, in distresses for Christ's sake: for when I am weak, then am I strong.

II Corinthians, ch. 12, vs 9–10

THE contents of this book were not couched in profound language, neither were they carefully contrived and arranged by its author for publication as a book. This book is just a collection of articles written under the running title 'The Great and Terrible Day of the Lord'. It is an unfinished symphony, for their author went to glory leaving the greater part of his tale untold, and many of his articles (chapters twelve to nineteen) unpublished and still in manuscript form.

It is true that when these articles were first published in the magazine *Bible Truth* (of which Rev. C. S. McKelvey was an editor) a few wrote complaining that they were the idle ramblings of an old man who should have retired gracefully long since, while some wrote railing against the message which they contained. However, a great majority wrote telling of their heartfelt gratitude to the Lord for insight, uplift or some other spiritual edification received while reading them. It has been the continuing encouragement and support of these latter (who had regard to the spirit of the message and not to the letters which contained it) which has led to the publication of this book.

Weak in expression and construction it may be, for it constitutes the writings of a man in his eighties, much written in the weeks just prior to his death. Its strength lies in the fact that it represents the last words of prophetic interpretation from a man greatly blessed and used by the Lord in this ministry for more than fifty years. As such it merits prayerful consideration, for the reader must ask himself whether the old stalwart, as he neared the very end of his earthly pilgrimage, could see more clearly the meaning of those things from above which are contained in the prophetic writings of the Bible.

During his long and active life the Rev. Charles Samuel McKelvey wrote and published thousands of pages on the interpretation of the prophetic scriptures, including hundreds of magazine articles and several booklets (notably, *A Balanced Gospel for Today,* and *The Bible, History, and Britain*), but he never published a book. It was not in his nature to write a book. He always said that he had not got the patience for it, and that he was happy to leave that job to others. The truth is that Mac (as he was affectionately known to so many) was not a writer. Above all he was a very gifted public speaker; an able, intensely absorbing, witty and profound teacher of the oracles of God revealed in the Bible. Whatever the occasion, conference address or front room Bible study, Mac was always sublimely at ease with his congregation as he led them to see things from God's point of view, and he was never more happy than when speaking of the things of God. He was a natural man of the people, but he was not a natural man of the pen. The necessary constraints of writing (its slowness, its grammatical demands) and the lack of a living congregation made writing a chore for him. In fact, Mac never really submitted to its discipline. Instead he would crank out his monthly article on his battered old typewriter, almost devoid of full-stops and commas, and composed of unending sentences like a Pauline epistle. He would use exactly the same form of words as if he were speaking, and would quote each scripture from memory (usually with all the right words, and invariably with the wrong punctuation) but forgetting to give the reference. In short, the finished product was an editor's nightmare when,

INTRODUCTION

without further attention from Mac, it arrived on his desk. The editor would then spend longer transforming and translating the article into a form suitable for publication than Mac had in writing it!

Throughout his ministry Mac was blessed with friends willing and able to spend long hours interpreting him to, and for, his readers. For many years Mr. Parrot, the editor of *Brith,* performed this arduous task, and it is only right that he and the others should be recognised, for, as Mac would have been the first to admit, without them his articles would never have reached their world-wide audience. I believe the editors were aided by the Lord in their task, for they somehow managed to preserve in the finished product Mac's personality and expression while often completely rewriting and rearranging his phrases, sentences, and sometimes whole paragraphs. This description of the manner by which Mac's articles reached their public is not revealed in order to belittle Mac, far from it. It is made public because it is true, and of interest, and mainly so that his readers can pause and consider the manner of God's working with men, in that He gave revelation to one man, who wrote it down with untidy excitement, and patience to another, who ensured that it reached those who wanted it in a form suitable for their proper edification.

In reading this book those that knew Mac will no doubt enjoy again his standpoint and mode of expression, because it will carry them back and away to those often sublime occasions when they sat enthralled and oblivious to time as he unfolded and explained the Bible to them. However, for those who never heard him preach, some few further words of explanation might be helpful.

Mac was thoroughly at home in the Bible. For him there was no credibility gap between what the Bible said and what he believed it meant. If it strained human credibility to accept the Divine revelation he simply abandoned human reasoning and left the Divine author to work it out. (It is usually far harder for the Lord to deal with human credibility than to perform His prophetic word!) He did not try and work it out for the Lord by inventing some lesser and more acceptable fulfilment. Instead he stood firmly and unshakably on the full, exact and natural meaning of the Bible's words.

Moreover, for Mac there was no gap between the world of the Bible and the world of nations, newspapers and international affairs. Bible prophecy predicted the future of the nations, while newspapers described the fulfilments. It should be understood of course that he lived in the world of the Bible rather than in the one described in the newspapers, for he was completely persuaded which of the two gave him the truest account of what was going on in the world, and the clearest view of its future. Certainly he was very much in the world, but he was definitely not of it. He lived in, and was of, that world ever inhabited by the prophets who perceive clearly the reality of those angelic beings, the princes who stand for nations, the hand of evil manipulating the nations of the ungodly, and the arm of the Lord, ever victorious, fulfilling His purpose throughout the centuries and through His people Israel. So he always interpreted the newspapers in the light of the Bible rather than making the common mistake of trying to do the reverse. In his mind he perceived the nations only according to their correct biblical names, titles and origins, and he would often so name them in conversation, in preaching and when writing. In everyday conversation he would often refer to the Arabians as 'Ishmael', to Russia as 'the king of the north', to the U.S.A. as 'Manasseh', and to Great Britain as 'Ephraim'. Likewise, the use of Bible symbols was a natural component of his teaching. Thus, he mystified the ignorant, bored the fool, but delighted the seeker after truth by his talk of beasts, fig trees, and ten-toed nations! And yet, the thinking man must pause to ask himself whether the Bible is far wrong in symbolising nations in this way. Is there not something intensely beastly about the actions of ungodly nations and their leaders? I feel Mac was right, who saw the world as God sees it, and others, who would ignore the beastliness of godless politics and rose-tint the idolatrous humanism of man's self-worship, are deluded and wrong. So no apology need be made to the reader for Mac's uninhibited use of the rich symbolism of the prophets throughout the articles which make up this book. Any reader who does not readily understand is advised not to discard this book as incomprehensible, but rather to strive to gain understanding of the Bible's language which leads to clear sightedness.

It was not widely recognised during his lifetime, but it was true, that Mac was unique with respect to the interpretation of Bible prophecy, for his teaching did not fit into any of the neat little pigeon-holes which describe the various major schools of thought. His teaching contained strong elements of three schools of prophetic thought, namely, the historicist, the futurist, and especially the British Israelite school. To a large extent he was disowned by the 'purists' of all three schools because he was 'tainted' by the views of the other two. In fact he had the good sense to embrace the truth present in all three but to ignore the excesses of their exegeses where they distort scripture to fit the extremities of their dogmas. So, for instance, he did not view all history through the narrow embattled slit of the historicist which sees nothing but popery and the Pope, although he clearly understood the role of Rome as an antichrist force in history, but one whose days are numbered and whose force is now almost spent.

Neither was he a 'good' British Israelite! His teaching stressed the spiritual role of God's servant nation. In the days when the purists still loved to revel in the pomp and circumstance and the carnal trappings of empire he was teaching the coming recession of British power (now nearly complete). He had no time for the empty eggshells of earthly-mindedness.

Instead he emphasized only God's plans and His love for His people, showing that He was their only claim to greatness. He preached against personal and national sin and presented the Lord Jesus Christ as God's only answer. Thus, he preached the need for personal and national salvation and proclaimed his belief in the power of the blood of Jesus to accomplish both.

Often he was accused of being a futurist, though no self-respecting futurist would hold with most of his teaching! Certainly Mac taught that there would be fulfilments in the near future of prophecies which historicists regard as cast-iron examples of prophecy totally fulfilled long ago. Yet Mac had no quarrel with these opponents for he recognised fully the historical fulfilment. Where Mac stood apart in his interpretation was in recognising more fully than most the amazing circular movements in history whereby events repeat themselves and circumstances reshape almost exactly as before, so that prophecy can have double and even multiple real fulfilments. So he contended that others were often mistaken in teaching the total and final fulfilment of a prophecy just because there had already been one absolutely real outworking in history of its predictions. Thus, Mac could accept that the popes were antichrists while still looking for the antichrist to appear among Jewry in Palestine just before the Second Coming of the Lord Jesus Christ. I believe he was right, and I believe that the interpretation of prophecy given in the Bible by the apostolic preachers used the selfsame approach. So Peter, on the day of Pentecost, could take a prophecy from Joel which is widely understood to have a still future fulfilment just before the great and terrible day of the Lord ('The sun shall be turned into darkness, and the moon into blood, before that great and notable day of the Lord come:' Acts, ch. 2, v. 20) and say, 'But this is that which was spoken by the prophet Joel', (v. 16), referring to the outpouring of God's Holy Spirit which had occurred that very day. Clearly, Joel chapter two, verses

INTRODUCTION

twenty-eight to thirty-two had one fulfilment on the day of Pentecost (which pleases the historicists) and it must yet have another fulfilment (which will please the futurists). Mac was always pleased to accept both fulfilments and believed that a large proportion of prophecy contained the essential promise of more than one real fulfilment. ('And as it was in the days of Noe, so shall it be also in the days of the Son of man.' – Luke, ch. 17, v. 26.) Failure to recognise the truth of two parallel, real fulfilments is the major stumbling block between those who see only the more widely accepted fulfilment of many prophecies in the person of God's servant (the Lord Jesus Christ), and those who see their fulfilment only in God's servant nation (Israel), and this failure has fired many heated exchanges between British Israelites and others. Here too, Mac saw that both are so right. He fully believed that all God's promises are yea and Amen in Him (the Lord Jesus Christ) since all the covenants are invested in His person. However, that did not stop him understanding the full reality of God's unchanging love for His chosen nation and the absolute necessity that they also fulfil His prophetic word and covenant promises. Just as a real fulfilment of so much in Christ demands the earthly existence, growth and functioning of His body the Church, so any real fulfilment of much else demands the unbroken continuance of the earthly ministry of His blind servant nation of Israel. It has been said that, "In the land of the blind, a one-eyed man is king." Thank God for all who still truly believe in any real fulfilment of prophecy, but thank God the more for one who saw God's prophetic truth with both eyes open!

Mac's teaching was so much more than the sum of the parts of the other schools of interpretation which he accepted, for added to them was a unique insight into the mind of the Almighty best described as a revelation. The whole was crowned by his outgoing personality. Unlike most savants he was not a remote, obscure scholar, rarely available and then only to those who fully appreciated his teaching. He was, as so many know, a man constantly available, seemingly with endless time to spare, and very ready to give practical help to people of all sorts and conditions, both believers and unbelievers.

Much more could be written about his humour, courage and other attractive qualities but he would not wish it. Were he here, he would allow no time for speaking about himself or his teaching but would launch directly into one more glorious exposition of the Scriptures and their revelation of his Lord. He would long since be impatient to begin teaching! So in deference to his memory I will end this introduction and direct the reader immediately to chapter one.

MICHAEL DAVID BENNETT
Cambridge, 1979

NOTES CONCERNING BIBLICAL QUOTES

Italics	Indicates author's emphasis
[ ]	Brackets actually occurring in the A.V.
( )	Author's or other authorities' explanations

Chapter 1

FUTURE FIGURES IN FOCUS

WHEN we think of the First Coming of the Lord, we do not think so much of the day of His birth, but of the thirty-four years of His life-span on the earth. We begin, in fact, in the Temple with Zacharias being told by the angel that he would have a son who would be the forerunner of the Lord. From this standpoint we go on speaking about the First Coming of the Lord until His ascension into heaven.

In the same way we must think of the Second Coming of the Lord as a series of events starting before He descends from heaven in bodily form, and continuing for a period after the actual return. In fact, the Lord said in Luke chapter seventeen, verse twenty-two:

> 'The days will come, when ye shall desire to see one of the days of the Son of man, and ye shall not see it.'

We often mistakenly think of prophecy as always being fulfilled by a most miraculous event, when often it is fulfilled quite naturally, and in such a way that we do not notice its importance. The Second Coming of the Lord is a period that started in 1917 with the taking of Jerusalem. At this time prophecy was fulfilled by the British taking the city without a shot being fired as the Turks suddenly took fright and moved out of the city. This was the end of the Gentile rule of Jerusalem and so a major prophecy passed into history (Luke, ch. 21, v. 24).

> 'Jerusalem shall be trodden down of the Gentiles, until the times of the Gentiles be fulfilled.'

The Christian Church hardly noticed, that prophecy had been fulfilled, and certainly Israel-Britain did not see that she was

Israel. She would not know this, for her own good, until a much later date (Romans, ch. 11, v. 25):

> 'For I would not, brethren, that ye should be ignorant of this mystery, lest ye should be wise in your own conceits; that blindness in part is happened to Israel, until the fulness of the Gentiles be come in.'

The realisation by Israel-Britain of her identity is an event which must occur prior to the Coming of the Lord, and is yet well in the future.

Another event pointing to the Lord's Coming occurred in 1948 when the Israeli nation was born in a day. At that time the Israelis took over half the city of Jerusalem, and that was the business half (Zephaniah, ch. 1, v. 11). They did not take the Holy Place in 1948; this came in 1967 which was another milestone towards the Coming of the Lord.

We now follow another series of events described in the four horses of Revelation chapter six. The first horse is white, symbolising the time of the beginning of the end when the Lord Jesus Christ first comes unseen into the picture of the end time. This horse is the only one with a rider that wins:

> 'And I saw, and behold a white horse: and he that sat on him had a bow; and a crown was given unto him: and he went forth conquering, and to conquer.'
>
> Revelation, ch. 6, v. 2

It is interesting to note that the 'bow' is Judah and the 'arrows' are Ephraim (Zechariah, ch. 9, v. 13).

The second horse is red and symbolises a military power. This horse began to operate in 1945. Since then nearly every change of government has been a military take-over. For instance, nearly every state in Africa is controlled by the armed forces. The red horse, like the others, stays in operation until the great battle of the Lord. Its rider has power 'to take peace from the earth, and that they should kill one another: and there was given unto him a great sword.' (Revelation, ch. 6, v. 4).

The third horse is now in the picture and the rider is well in

FUTURE FIGURES IN FOCUS

the saddle. This is the black horse whose rider has a pair of scales in his hand symbolising the economic power. This horse even now is controlling the price of food and of every other need of the people. It is causing rising prices at a time when even governments have to spend more time considering the price of butter, sugar, and bread than almost any other national problem. It is comforting to know that the power of this rider is limited to the Gentile world and cannot win against Israel-Britain. Although we too are suffering now with inflation, we will not suffer like the other nations.

The fourth horse is not yet fully prepared and is yet future. From the Bible standpoint, he has not yet got the rider on him. However, it cannot be long now before this pale horse and its rider, the deadliest of the three, will be loose on the earth. We know that this horse represents communism. Communism is well established over at least half of the world, but, as yet, it is riderless. Prophetically this horse does not operate fully until the prince of Gog and Magog is in control. It is interesting to see that the black horse is used by God to bring down the pale horse, the communistic horse of death, but this subject will be studied later.

We now turn to Daniel chapter two and see there the four great empires of Nebuchadnezzar's dream and its interpretation by God through Daniel. The four empires were Babylon, Medo-Persia, Greece and Rome. We are not interested here in the first three, for they are all past; but we are interested in the last stage of the fourth power – Rome. This stage represents the present time when the Roman Church is still in control but is now nearing its end. According to Daniel there is to appear a grouping of all these four great empires under Russia, which was never one of the four. These four will be under their new names: Irak, Iran, Greece and Italy, making the final Babylon that we read about in the Daniel image. Thus, Daniel said there would be five empires. This last conglomeration of parallel empires will be destroyed by being hit by the 'stone' kingdom:

> 'Then was the iron, the clay, the brass, the silver, and the gold, broken to pieces together, and became like the chaff of the summer threshing-floors; and the wind carried them away, that no place was found for them:'
>
> Daniel, ch. 2, v. 35

It will fall into crushed dust and be seen no more. It will be crushed by the Lord Jesus Christ in the great judgment when He comes to take over all the kingdoms of this world.

Rome was the fourth empire, and was to have seven heads or seven forms of government. Five existed before the birth of the Lord, so when He was born the sixth was ruling. The position was still the same when John wrote the book of Revelation. The five forms of government that fell before the end of the B.C. age were Kings, Consuls, Dictators, Decemvirs and Triumvirs, and the sixth was the Emperors.

> 'And here is the mind which hath wisdom. The seven heads are seven mountains, on which the woman sitteth. And there are seven kings: five are fallen, and one is, and the other is not yet come; and when he cometh, he must continue a short space.'
>
> Revelation, ch. 17, vs 9–10

The seventh that was still future in St. John's day is Rome under the Pope, or Ecclesiastical Rome. Thus Rome is described elsewhere in the same chapter:

> '... and I saw a woman sit upon a scarlet coloured beast, full of names of blasphemy, having seven heads and ten horns. And the woman was arrayed in purple (the colour of kings) and scarlet colour (the colour of the priestly office), and decked with gold and precious stones and pearls, having a golden cup in her hand full of abominations and filthiness of her fornication: And upon her forehead was a name written, MYSTERY, BABYLON THE GREAT, THE MOTHER OF HARLOTS AND ABOMINATIONS OF THE EARTH. And I saw the woman drunken with the blood of the saints, and with the blood of the martyrs of Jesus: (the 16th century, the time of the Inquisition) and when I saw her, I wondered with great admiration. And the angel said unto me, Wherefore didst thou marvel? I will tell thee the mystery of the woman, and of the beast that carrieth her, which hath the seven heads and ten horns.'
>
> Revelation, ch. 17, vs 3–7

Rome as the Roman Church is the last form of the power of 'BABYLON THE GREAT', the great power of the Gentile world which was set up at Babel to oppose the Lord and His Kingdom on earth (Israel). The historical Babylon will soon come to its end. It is finished by the ten horns on the beast.

> 'And he saith unto me, The waters which thou sawest, where the whore sitteth, are peoples, and multitudes, and nations, and tongues. And the ten horns which thou sawest upon the beast, these shall hate the whore, and shall make her desolate and naked, and shall eat her flesh, and burn her with fire. . . . And the woman which thou sawest is that great city, which reigneth over the kings of the earth.'
>
> Revelation, ch. 17, vs 15, 16 and 18

The 'ten horns' which are the last remnant of the old Roman Empire represent Germany, France, Italy, Spain, Portugal, Hungary, Austria, Czechoslovakia, Greece and Turkey. These nations are all going to become communist, and therefore anti-God. For a time after the fall of Rome these will stand as independent communistic states, very friendly with Russia, who exercises great influence over them until eventually they readily agree to be governed by Russia. The short period of independent rule by the 'ten horns' is made quite plain:

> 'And the ten horns which thou sawest are ten kings, which have received no kingdom as yet; but receive power as kings one hour with the beast. These have one mind, and shall give their power and strength unto the beast.'
>
> Revelation, ch. 17, vs 12–13

This is the time when the beast appears to be dead, for it receives a deadly wound at the time of the fall of the Roman Church. That mighty beast has only ten horns, but it reappears, more diabolical than ever, this time with three evil powers ruling it.

> 'And I saw one of his heads as it were wounded to death; and his deadly wound was healed: and all the world wondered after the beast. And they worshipped the dragon which gave power unto the beast: and they worshipped the beast, saying, Who is like unto the beast? who is able to make war with him?'
>
> Revelation, ch. 13, vs 3–4

When we see in prophecy the might of Russia governing the whole of Europe and only the British Isles against it, we see the coming challenge, for it will seem to the world as if we are really doomed. However, our trust will be in the Lord, and from the Lord's standpoint, Russia and all her allies are really very weak, for He says: (Isaiah, ch. 40, v. 15):

> 'Behold, the nations are as a drop of a bucket, and are counted as the small dust of the balance: behold, he taketh up the isles as a very little thing.'

The dragon is Satan, the arch-enemy of the Lord and of Israel.

> 'And I saw an angel come down from heaven, having the key of the bottomless pit and a great chain in his hand. And he laid hold on the dragon, that old serpent, which is the Devil, and Satan, and bound him a thousand years,'
>
> Revelation, ch. 20, vs 1–2

There is a work that only Satan can do. The beast system cannot do it but Satan must do this work through the beast, thus the two powers emerge. Now for the third power:

> 'And I beheld another beast coming up out of the earth; and he had two horns like a lamb, and he spake as a dragon.'
>
> Revelation, ch. 13, v. 11

The lamb-like person is evil and does all the things that the beast does, he has two horns, therefore he is both a secular leader and an evil spiritual leader as well. Thus we see three evil heads in the final stage of the Babylonian System.

Prophecy is given to the end that, when it comes to pass, we might believe. If we know the prophecies, we have our faith in the Lord, and keep our confidence in Him when they happen. If we don't know the prophecies then we can be badly shaken in our faith as we see everything apparently going wrong. We should, therefore, get a fairly clear picture of what the Bible tells us concerning future events just before they really take place. We now have to turn to Revelation chapter sixteen:

> 'And I saw three unclean spirits like frogs come out of the mouth of the dragon, and out of the mouth of the beast, and out of the mouth of the false prophet. For they are the spirits of devils, working miracles, which go forth unto the kings of the earth and of the whole world, to gather them to the battle of that great day of God Almighty.'
>
> Revelation, ch. 16, vs 13–14

We have already seen that 'the dragon' is Satan; that 'the beast' is the final leader of the final state of Babylon; and therefore, 'the false prophet' is the two-horned lamb. They all three go out to try God's people Israel and Judah, and to enslave the nations of the world: but, like so many evil plotters, their evil plans are turned upon themselves. These three evil powers will be used by God to bring all the nations of the world to Jerusalem to battle in that great day when the Lord Jesus Christ comes to begin His reign upon the earth.

So far we have seen what the Lord tells us about many nations, but we still have to consider all the nations in the Middle East who might otherwise appear to be outside of the world-wide plan of God.

We read in Daniel that when the Russians come down into Palestine the 'king of the south' shall push at him. The king of the south brings in Arabia which plays a minor role. The true Arabs, who are the descendants of Ishmael, will never accept communism. They are fatalists, who believe in one God, but in accordance with the Koran they believe that Christ was a prophet who will one day return to the earth, to Mecca, their sacred city. The king of the south (the Arabs) will try to oppose the advancing Russian armies but will be swept to one side.

So we now turn to Isaiah chapter 46 (verses 10–11):

> '... My counsel shall stand, and I will do all my pleasure: Calling a ravenous bird from the east, the man that executeth my counsel from a far country: yea, I have spoken it, I will also bring it to pass; I have purposed it, I will also do it.'

We look for the identity of this bird and find the answer in the verse just before the one dealing with the three unclean spirits:

> 'And the sixth angel poured out his vial upon the great river Euphrates; and the water thereof was dried up, that the way of the kings of the east might be prepared.'
>
> Revelation, ch. 16, v. 12

Thus, we see that the ravenous bird from the east is the communist leader of China gathering the nations of the Far East to Palestine to the great battle of the Lord. We know this looks complicated but it will become quite plain when, in the coming chapters, we look at each one of the powers separately and see their roles, each one different from the others, but each one being massed by Satan to destroy Israel and to defeat the Lord when He comes. Satan is stirring up the world in hatred against the Lord. We see this quite plainly in Revelation chapter eleven (vs 15 and 18):

> 'And the seventh angel sounded; and there were great voices in heaven, saying, The kingdoms of this world are become the kingdoms of our Lord, and of his Christ; and he shall reign for ever and ever. . . . And the nations were angry, and thy wrath is come, and the time of the dead, that they should be judged. . . .'

Again, we turn to another passage of the Scriptures and read that all the Gentile nations will be joined together in one great conference, with only one item on the agenda (Psalm 2, vs 1–3):

> 'Why do the heathen rage, and the people imagine a vain thing? The kings of the earth set themselves, and the rulers take counsel together, against the LORD, and against his anointed, saying, Let us break their bands asunder, and cast away their cords from us.'

With all this in mind we see there will never be another world war like the last two, moreover we can well rule out atomic war also.

Having paved the way for the coming chapters that will deal in detail with all these prophecies, we must look on the other side, and see what is prophesied as happening to the Israel nations – the peoples of Great Britain, and Ireland, together with Canada, U.S.A., Southern Africa, Australia and New Zealand, and also the Israel groups living just the other side of the Channel, who will eventually come over to these Islands when Russia dominates Europe, to be received with open arms by their kinsmen of Israel. The seven nations listed above will form one solid front against the common foe, and will all come under the Throne of David. We of Israel will not even worry about our foes with all their boastings because we will be safe in our 'Chambers', and the Lord will be our defence and protection. Psalm 46 is the answer:

> 'God is our refuge and strength, a very present help in trouble. Therefore will not we fear, though the earth be removed, and though the mountains be carried into the midst of the sea: . . .
> The heathen raged, the kingdoms were moved: he uttered his voice, the earth melted. The LORD of hosts is with us; the God of Jacob is our refuge.'
>
> Psalm 46, vs 1, 6 and 7

The Lord invites us not to fear but to see the great work which He is doing. We can take an interest in every stage if we know what the operation is, and how it is going to bring health to the world. So the Lord says to us, 'come and see'; just like a brilliant surgeon, who knowing that the operation will be a success, might ask a friend to watch the process.

> 'Come, behold the works of the LORD, what desolations he hath made in the earth. He maketh wars to cease unto the end of the earth; he breaketh the bow, and cutteth the spear in sunder; he burneth the chariot in the fire.'
>
> Psalm 46, vs 8 and 9

However, before this can happen, God must be acknowledged by the whole of the human race. In fact when God is in His right place He will put the whole world in its proper place before Him. While He is performing this gigantic operation we must be calm and confident. So the Psalm ends with the words:

> 'Be still, and know that I am God: I will be exalted among the heathen, I will be exalted in the earth. The LORD of hosts is with us; the God of Jacob is our refuge.'

Chapter 2

SATAN AND THE FOURFOLD DEFENCE OF ISRAEL

SO FAR in our studies we have seen that, in the last stages before the Coming of the Lord, there will be several evil powers all of which the Lord will draw into the battle of the great day of the Lord. We have listed these as:
(a) the dragon, or Satan,
(b) the beast headed by the chief prince of Gog and Magog,
(c) the lamb-like beast with two horns, or the false prophet,
(d) the evil bird from the east, and,
(e) the king of the south.

We now have to deal with each of these in turn, and so, we start with Satan. He has a work to do that cannot be done by any of the others. Satan alone can attack Israel, and so we read in Revelation chapter twelve that the time comes when Satan will be cast out of heaven shortly before the return of the Lord.

> 'Therefore rejoice, ye heavens, and ye that dwell in them. Woe to the inhabiters of the earth and of the sea! for the devil is come down unto you, having great wrath, because he knoweth that he hath but a short time.' (v. 12)

Now go to verse fifteen:

> 'And the serpent cast out of his mouth water as a flood after the woman (Israel), that he might cause her to be carried away of the flood. And the earth helped the woman, and the earth opened her mouth, and swallowed up the flood which the dragon cast out of his mouth.'

This flood, coming out of the serpent's mouth, is a form of propaganda. It is called a flood to show the magnitude of the wave. Already we see the communist attack becoming more and more serious. There are communist leaders in nearly every walk of life and dominating every section of the community to which they belong. A few communist leaders cause endless trouble in the trade unions. In the colleges they cause riots; and so we could go on. Even the government is under the sway of the leftists. It only needs Parliament to come under the control of a communistic element to cause havoc in the nation. Satan is now so active that this attack could come this year. According to Isaiah chapter fourteen, Satan says that he 'will sit also upon the mount of the congregation, in the sides of the north':

> 'For thou hast said in thine heart, I will ascend into heaven, I will exalt my throne above the stars of God: I will sit also upon the mount of the congregation, in the sides of the north.'
> Isaiah, ch. 14, v. 13

This can mean only one thing. Satan will try to cause the Queen or her successor to abdicate, or be dethroned. Instead of a monarch he will try to place the nation under a communist leader. Satan must try to destroy the British Throne. It must be one of his prime objectives because it is the Throne of David which is being held by the house of David for the Lord Jesus Christ. Of course, he will fail.

Satan seems to be winning all along the line with what he is doing. He hopes and intends to destroy us, for if he can do so, the Lord Jesus Christ will have to come and curse the whole world. I would not dare write this were it not the Word of God:

> 'Behold, I will send you Elijah the prophet before the coming of the great and dreadful day of the LORD: And he shall turn the heart of the fathers to the children, and the heart of the children to their fathers, lest I come and smite the earth with a curse.'
> Malachi, ch. 4, vs 5–6

It is a most terrible thought that, if we do not return to the Lord, then the whole world will be cursed instead of being blessed. Satan must and will fail.

Satan has already been most successful in the visible Church. He appears in several disguises, 'as a roaring lion . . .

seeking whom he may devour' (I Peter, ch. 5, v. 8), but in the Church he is 'an angel of light'.

> 'But what I do, that I will do, that I may cut off occasion from them which desire occasion; that wherein they glory, they may be found even as we. For such are false apostles, deceitful workers, transforming themselves into the apostles of Christ. And no marvel; for Satan himself is transformed into an angel of light. Therefore it is no great thing if his ministers also be transformed as the ministers of righteousness; whose end shall be according to their works.'
> II Corinthians, ch. 11, vs 12–15

Many of the ministers of today believe they are serving the Lord, but they are really blind servants of Satan, working havoc in the congregations with their false modernistic teachings. O for a strong-willed man like St. Paul, who would have none of them or their teaching!

We are seeing ourselves being humbled by our leaders who believe that we are finished as a world power. Our economic troubles show that we are paying a very high price for their belief in the Common Market. As soon as Germany, France and Italy find that we are unable to pay, they will turn on us with all their hatred. We are seeing our government going from bad to worse. In trying to make peace with the trade union leaders they are paying out their, or rather our, money in an unsuccessful attempt to keep prices down. We are seeing share prices falling more than ever before and businesses going bankrupt. The industrial world has no faith whatever in the politicians' control, whose only stock in trade is words, words, words. The government has no hope of getting the country out of the mess which it is getting into.

The Bible student is far more optimistic, for he is told in the Bible that it is the time of 'Jacob's trouble'. We can be quite sure of the future, for the passage goes on to say: 'but he shall be saved out of it' – not 'from it' but 'out of it'.

> 'Alas! for that day is great, so that none is like it: it is even the time of Jacob's trouble; but he shall be saved out of it.'
> Jeremiah, ch. 30, v. 7

We are certainly going through Jacob's trouble now but we have not yet come to the climax. We may see the climax during 1975 or it may be the years after, but when our trouble has served its purpose, first, in bringing us out of the world, second, in making us see our hopelessness and the fact that we cannot do anything to help ourselves, then we will turn back to our God. Then we shall see the works of the Lord and how He is saving us from ourselves and the results of our evil ways, and bringing us out of our troubles and back to Himself. If the Lord were to bless us as we are now, He would be confirming us in all the evil ways of our permissive society.

That we will turn to our God in our great need is both sure and certain!
Psalm 79, v. 9:

> 'Help us, O God of our salvation, for the glory of thy name: and deliver us, and purge away our sins, for thy name's sake.'

And in Jeremiah, ch. 31, v. 18:

> 'I have surely heard Ephraim bemoaning himself thus; Thou hast chastised me, and I was chastised, as a bullock unaccustomed to the yoke: turn thou me, and I shall be turned; for thou art the LORD my God.'

The Lord has said, 'No weapon that is formed against thee shall prosper' (Isaiah, ch. 54, v. 17). In fact, the Lord will not proceed with His judgments in the world until He has made us absolutely safe. I want to make this absolutely plain before going on to write about the judgments that are to come upon the world. Our safety and protection from the world-wide hatred that will be against us is assured by the Word of God. First, the Lord will bring us out of our involvement in Europe and NATO. He will bring us into absolute isolation from all the Gentile nations by bringing us under His divine command, and in that day we will be willing to do His will.

'Come, my people, enter thou into thy chambers, and shut thy doors about thee: hide thyself as it were for a little moment, until the indignation be overpast. For, behold, the LORD cometh out of his place to punish the inhabitants of the earth for their iniquity: the earth also shall disclose her blood, and shall no more cover her slain.'
Isaiah, ch. 26, vs 20–21

Let me make this quite clear. God is neither like a doting father saving a weakling child, nor is He treating Israel like a chosen people. The real position is that the world is divided into two sections. Israel was taken from among the Gentiles, from the Adamic stock to form the first part of the Kingdom of God on earth. Israel as a nation has been trained in the bitter school of experience, and will be until she becomes fit to lead the rest of the nations into the Kingdom of God under the rulership of the Lord Jesus Christ. Until then, all the other nations must remain in the 'principality of darkness' under the rule of Satan. When the Lord comes this rule will end, but, Satan will try to retain it.

We have come to the beginning of the final struggle between God and Satan, and therefore, the fight between good and evil must be fought out without mercy. Satan will try to keep all the nations under his control, and he must try to destroy Israel, the Kingdom of God on earth. However, the Lord will take all the Adamic race away from Satan and enchain him in the 'bottomless pit' for a thousand years. Therefore Satan will bring the forces of evil, including all the evil angels, into the struggle ready for a last attempt to subdue or destroy Israel. On the other hand, all the greed, the desire for power, and revenge and all the other evil and unworthy instincts of man must go, never to return again.

Israel and the Church are Satan's targets in this last stage, and therefore the Lord, with the peace of the whole world at stake, will protect His own and will not move until He has made Israel absolutely safe. When Satan sees that his attack by the use of the flood has failed, and that he cannot subdue Israel, he will try to exterminate them. So we read:

> 'And the earth helped the woman (Israel), and the earth opened her mouth, and swallowed up the flood which the dragon cast out of his mouth. And the dragon was wroth with the woman, and went to make war with the remnant of her seed. . . .'
> Revelation, ch. 12, vs 16–17

Satan, however, will not even start the war on Israel in the Islands, for they are safe in their Chambers.

The next defence of Israel is seen in Revelation chapter seven:

> 'And after these things I saw four angels standing on the four corners of the earth, holding the four winds of the earth, that the wind should not blow on the earth, nor on the sea, nor on any tree. And I saw another angel ascending from the east, having the seal of the living God: and he cried with a loud voice to the four angels, to whom it was given to hurt the earth and the sea, Saying, Hurt not the earth, neither the sea, nor the trees, till we have sealed the servants of our God in their foreheads. And I heard the number of them which were sealed: and there were sealed an hundred and forty and four thousand of all the tribes of the children of Israel.'
> Revelation. ch. 7, vs 1–4

Sodom and Gomorrah could have been saved from destruction if ten righteous men had been found in those cities. They would have been a covering under which the cities could be sheltered by the Lord. Likewise, the Lord could only save Israel from destruction if there were a number of the faithful in the land. So in Romans we read:

> 'God hath not cast away his people which he foreknew. Wot ye not what the scripture saith of Elias? how he maketh intercession to God against Israel, saying, Lord, they have killed thy prophets, and digged down thine altars; and I am left alone, and they seek my life. But what saith the answer of God unto him? I have reserved to myself seven thousand men, who have not bowed the knee to the image of Baal.'
> Romans, ch. 11, vs 2–4

Seven thousand men about whom the prophet knew nothing. They may have been in hiding for fear of being caught by the priests of Baal, but they were a covering so that the Lord could be merciful to Israel; so likewise now, there must be those people selected to cover us. They must be believers in the Lord Jesus Christ; they must believe the whole of the Word of God to be true from cover to cover; they will not know who they are; they may not be publicly witnessing, only fully believing. In Matthew a distinction is made which is worth noting:

> 'And except those days should be shortened, there should no flesh be saved: but for the elect's sake those days shall be shortened. Then if any man shall say unto you, Lo, here is Christ, or there; believe it not. For there shall arise false Christs, and false prophets, and shall shew great signs and wonders; insomuch that, if it were possible, they shall deceive the very elect.'
>
> Matthew, ch. 24, vs 22–24

Here the Lord shows that 'the elect' can be deceived but that the 'very elect' cannot be deceived. Therefore, it is reasonable to assume that the 'very elect' are those whom God has sealed for the covering of His people. These words also show how great the danger is, that so many must be sealed.

First we saw the Chambers of safety; second we saw the sealed one hundred and forty-four thousand. Now we must see defence number three:

> 'And at that time shall Michael stand up, the great prince which standeth for the children of thy people: and there shall be a time of trouble, such as never was since there was a nation even to that same time: and at that time thy people shall be delivered, every one that shall be found written in the book.'
>
> Daniel, ch. 12, v. 1

It seems as if these three safety precautions come into operation one after another as the situation becomes more intense, and then comes the ultimate defence that takes place near the return of the Lord and finalises in His return. Isaiah chapter fifty-nine presents our confession of our hopeless plight; we have turned away from our God and our sins have made the Lord to turn His face from us so that He will not hear; then follows the indictment against us and our resulting plight.

> '. . . we wait for light, but behold obscurity; for brightness, but we walk in darkness. We grope for the wall like the blind, and we grope as

if we had no eyes: we stumble at noonday as in the night; we are in desolate places as dead men . . . In transgressing and lying against the LORD, and departing away from our God. . . .'
Isaiah, ch. 59, vs 9–10 and 13

So it goes on, telling us just how hopeless we feel because we have departed from the Lord and His righteousness. Now follows the passage that gives us the assurance: He does not find a single political leader in Israel and not a single minister who can intercede for us. In our history there has always been a man to save us, but at this time there is no man forthcoming, and so:

'. . . he saw that there was no man, and wondered that there was no intercessor: therefore his arm brought salvation unto him. . . .'
Isaiah, ch. 59, v. 16

This most certainly applied when the Lord came from heaven to pay the price of sin, but in verses 19 to 21 it also applies to the future:

'So shall they fear the name of the LORD from the west, and his glory from the rising of the sun. When the enemy shall come in like a flood, the Spirit of the LORD shall lift up a standard against him (marginal reading – put him to flight). And the Redeemer shall come to Zion, and unto them that turn from transgression in Jacob, saith the LORD. As for me, this is my covenant with them, saith the LORD. My spirit that is upon thee, and my words which I have put in thy mouth, shall not depart out of thy mouth, nor out of the mouth of thy seed, nor out of the mouth of thy seed's seed, saith the LORD, from henceforth and for ever.'

Here then is the Lord's fourfold defence of His people.

Chapter 3

THE BOAST OF BABYLON – MOTHER AND DAUGHTER

WE MUST start this chapter by quoting at some length part of the remarkable second chapter of Daniel which gives us a clear prophetic summary of world history and its empires onwards from the time of Nebuchadnezzar, King of Babylon.

> 'Thou, O king, sawest, and behold a great image. This great image, whose brightness was excellent, stood before thee; and the form thereof was terrible. This image's head was of fine gold, his breast and his arms of silver, his belly and his thighs of brass, his legs of iron, his feet part of iron and part of clay.
>
> Thou sawest till that a stone was cut out without hands, which smote the image upon his feet that were of iron and clay, and brake them to pieces. Then was the iron, the clay, the brass, the silver, and the gold, broken to pieces together, and became like the chaff of the summer threshingfloors; and the wind carried them away, that no place was found for them: and the stone that smote the image became a great mountain, and filled the whole earth.
>
> This is the dream; and we will tell the interpretation thereof before the king. Thou, O king, art a king of kings: for the God of heaven hath given thee a kingdom, power, and strength, and glory.
>
> And wheresoever the children of men dwell, the beasts of the field and the fowls of the heaven hath he given into thine hand, and hath made thee ruler over them all. Thou art this head of gold. And after thee shall arise another kingdom inferior to thee, and another third kingdom of brass, which shall bear rule over all the earth. And the fourth kingdom shall be strong as iron: forasmuch as iron breaketh in pieces and subdueth all things: and as iron that breaketh all these, shall it break in pieces and bruise. And whereas thou sawest the feet and toes, part of potters' clay, and part of iron, the kingdom shall be divided; but there shall be in it of the strength of the iron, forasmuch as thou sawest the iron mixed with miry clay.
>
> And as the toes of the feet were part of iron, and part of clay, so the kingdom shall be partly strong, and partly broken.
>
> And whereas thou sawest iron mixed with miry clay, they shall mingle themselves with the seed of men: but they shall not cleave one to another, even as iron is not mixed with clay. And in the days of these

THE BOAST OF BABYLON – MOTHER AND DAUGHTER

kings shall the God of heaven set up a kingdom, which shall never be destroyed: and the kingdom shall not be left to other people, but it shall break in pieces and consume all these kingdoms, and it shall stand for ever. Forasmuch as thou sawest that the stone was cut out of the mountain without hands, and that it brake in pieces the iron, the brass, the clay, the silver, and the gold; the great God hath made known to the king what shall come to pass hereafter: and the dream is certain, and the interpretation thereof sure.'

Daniel, ch. 2, vs 31–45

In Daniel chapter two we read of the four successive great empires which began with Babylon under Nebuchadnezzar and will come to an end with the fall of the Roman Church. In order these were Babylon, Medo-Persia, Greece and Rome. Daniel's prophecy also tells of two other great empires which will arise after the collapse of the Roman Church. The first will be the final 'Babylonian' power which will cover the territories of all the four previous empires, namely, Iraq (Babylon), Iran (Persia), Greece and Rome. This empire will be allied with and recognise Russia as its head. The final power which Daniel saw is described as 'the stone . . . cut out of the mountain' (v. 45). The stone, which symbolises the Kingdom of God's Israel people, is seen to hit the image on the feet, so that the whole image is destroyed never to exist again. This 'stone' kingdom, goes on to fill the whole earth under the Kingship and reign of its great Corner Stone, the Lord Jesus Christ.

It is these last two great powers in which we are now interested. We have already seen that the Russian power will have two heads, namely, the dragon and the beast. The dragon (who is Satan) was the subject of chapter two. Now we have to study the beast power. The Holy Spirit tells us in Isaiah chapter thirteen of the Lord's challenge to Babylon in its final stage. The chapter opens with a simple statement that refers to the Coming of the Lord:

'The burden of Babylon, which Isaiah the son of Amoz did see. Lift ye up a banner upon the high mountain (the high mountain of Daniel ch. 2), exalt the voice unto them, shake the hand, that they may go into the gates of the nobles. I have commanded my sanctified ones, I have also called my mighty ones for mine anger, even them that rejoice in my highness. The noise of a multitude in the mountains, like as of a great people; a tumultuous noise of the kingdoms of nations gathered together: the LORD of hosts mustereth the host of the battle. They come from a far country, from the end of heaven, even the LORD, and the weapons of his indignation, to destroy the whole land (Palestine). Howl ye; for the day of the LORD is at hand; it shall come as a destruction from the Almighty.'

Isaiah, ch. 13, vs 1–6

We will study the rest of this chapter later, but we now turn to Isaiah chapter forty-seven and pick up the theme once more. Before we begin to study this chapter, we must notice that it is addressed to the 'virgin daughter of Babylon'.

'Come down, and sit in the dust, O virgin daughter of Babylon, sit on the ground: there is no throne, O daughter of the Chaldeans: for thou shalt no more be called tender and delicate.'

Isaiah, ch. 47, v. 1

The Hebrew word for 'virgin' here is 'bethular' meaning 'separation' (Young's Concordance). This is very enlightening as it shows that this Babylon is something new, and is separated from the historical Babylon, and is, in fact, the fifth empire that follows the fall of the Roman Church. There is no doubt that the first expression of Babylonian power was anything but what is described by the Hebrew word 'bethular'. Thus, Rome is described:

'... I will shew unto thee the judgment of the great whore that sitteth upon many waters: With whom the kings of the earth have committed fornication, and the inhabitants of the earth have been made drunk with the wine of her fornication. So he carried me away in the spirit into the wilderness: and I saw a woman sit upon a scarlet coloured beast, full of names of blasphemy, having seven heads and ten horns. And the woman was arrayed in purple and scarlet colour, and decked with gold and precious stones and pearls, having a golden cup in her hand full of abominations and filthiness of her fornication: And upon her forehead was a name written, MYSTERY, BABYLON THE GREAT, THE MOTHER OF HARLOTS AND ABOMINATIONS OF THE EARTH.'

Revelation, ch. 17, vs 1–5

THE BOAST OF BABYLON – MOTHER AND DAUGHTER

So much for Babylon the mother, but we are now considering 'the virgin daughter of Babylon'.

> 'Thy nakedness shall be uncovered, yea, thy shame shall be seen: I will take vengeance, and I will not meet thee as a man. As for our redeemer, the LORD of hosts is his name, the Holy One of Israel.'
> Isaiah, ch. 47, vs 3–4

This refers to the Coming of the Lord, and should give us confidence amid the things that are now taking place. Now comes the challenge of the Lord to Babylon:

> 'Sit thou silent, and get thee into darkness, O daughter of the Chaldeans: for thou shalt no more be called, The lady of kingdoms.'
> Isaiah, ch. 47, v. 5

Ever since the Lord divided the nations, and made Israel 'the people of God', and the Gentiles 'the kingdoms of this world' under Satan, Babylon has been 'The lady of kingdoms'.

> 'I was wroth with my people, I have polluted mine inheritance, and given them into thine hand: thou didst shew them no mercy; upon the ancient hast thou very heavily laid thy yoke.'
> Isaiah, ch. 47, v. 6

In Egypt, and during the captivities of Israel, this verse was fulfilled. In the case of Jewry it has also been fulfilled during the Christian Era, and still is being fulfilled. It is true of us now that we have surrendered ourselves into the hands of Europe and come under the Treaty of Rome. Thank the Lord that we shall be saved 'out of it'. Now comes the boasting of Babylon:

> 'And thou saidst, I shall be a lady for ever: so that thou didst not lay these things to thy heart, neither didst remember the latter end of it. Therefore hear now this, thou that art given to pleasures, that dwellest carelessly, that sayest in thine heart, I am, and none else beside me; I shall not sit as a widow, neither shall I know the loss of children.'
> Isaiah, ch. 47, vs 7–8

Israel has already experienced what Babylon claims she will never experience. Israel is a widow, having lost her husband when He died for her sins. She is called a widow in Isaiah (ch.

54, v. 4), 'Thou . . . shalt not remember the reproach of thy widowhood any more.' Israel has also lost her children. They have left us. However, the main boast of Babylon is in the name, 'I am, and none else beside me.' This boast takes the name that God gave Himself, when he became the Lord God of the nation of Israel at Sinai. By saying that there is 'none else beside me', they are repudiating the very existence of the Lord God Almighty. This boast is repeated in verse ten, when Babylon also states that, 'None seeth me'. Thus Babylon claims that there is no authority over her that can even know of her wickedness, let alone sit in judgment upon her.

> 'For thou hast trusted in thy wickedness: thou hast said, None seeth me. Thy wisdom and thy knowledge, it hath perverted thee; and thou hast said in thine heart, I am, and none else beside me.'
>
> Isaiah, ch. 47, v. 10

Thus, to summarise, the challenge of Babylon is:

(a) that she will never be a widow, or in other words, that Satan is her husband and she will be his wife for ever,

(b) that she will never lose her family, or in other words, once this great communistic control over all the nations takes place it will last for ever,

(c) that the godless state of the world will be subject to the rule of man and not subject to the overruling of the Lord.

Despite the confidence of these boasts, this Babylon will be brought down to the dust, because they have no reliable foundation. The boasts depend only on superstition:

> 'Stand now with thine enchantments, and with the multitude of thy sorceries, wherein thou hast laboured from thy youth; if so be thou shalt be able to profit, if so be thou mayest prevail. Thou art wearied in the multitude of thy counsels. Let now the astrologers, the stargazers, the monthly prognosticators, stand up, and save thee from these things that shall come upon thee.'
>
> Isaiah, ch. 47, vs 12–13

Now we go back to verse nine and see what will happen when God begins judgment on Babylon; and we see that the coming widowhood of Babylon is clearly stated in the Bible.

THE BOAST OF BABYLON – MOTHER AND DAUGHTER

> 'But these two things shall come to thee in a moment in one day, the loss of children, and widowhood: they shall come upon thee in their perfection (completeness) for the multitude of thy sorceries, and for the great abundance of thine enchantments.'
>
> Isaiah, ch. 47, v. 9

The fact is that these events will take place when the Lord returns. At that time Satan (and therefore Babylon) will lose all his power over all the tribes and nations because they will become 'the kingdoms of our Lord, and of his Christ' (Revelation, ch. 11, v. 15). First, Satan will be enchained in the bottomless pit for one thousand years, then he will be released for a little while, until the time comes for him to meet his final end.

> 'Forasmuch then as the children are partakers of flesh and blood, he also himself likewise took part of the same; that through death he might destroy him that had the power of death, that is, the devil.'
>
> Hebrews, ch. 2, v. 14

Israel has been enmeshed in the Babylonian set-up almost from her very beginning, and certainly in her captivities after which she came into these Islands. Then, by trading, and by making treaties with different parts of Babylon she has become further entangled. This has led her into wars and economic difficulties. However, the form of Babylon which we will have to face is the last stage of Babylon, and that is yet to come. It is described in the fourth horse and rider of Revelation (chapter six). We have already seen (see chapter one) that the first three riders are even now in the earth scene, but that the last has not yet gone forth. Of course, we can see quite plainly who the last horse will be, and how it is growing in strength all the time.

> 'And when he had opened the fourth seal, I heard the voice of the fourth beast say, Come and see. And I looked, and behold a pale horse: and his name that sat on him was Death, and Hell followed with him. And power was given unto them over the fourth part of the earth, to kill with sword, and with hunger, and with death, and with the beasts of the earth.'
>
> Revelation, ch. 6, vs 7–8

It is to cause her to escape from the terrible enactment of this, the Devil's worst crime against humanity, that the Lord says to Israel in no less than five passages in the Bible, that she must come out of Babylon as she (Babylon) begins to hold sway over the nations.

> 'Come, my people, enter thou into thy chambers, and shut thy doors about thee: hide thyself as it were for a little moment, until the indignation be overpast. For, behold, the LORD cometh out of his place to punish the inhabitants of the earth for their iniquity: the earth also shall disclose her blood, and shall no more cover her slain.'
>
> Isaiah, ch. 26, vs 20–21
>
> 'Go ye forth of Babylon, flee ye from the Chaldeans, with a voice of singing declare ye, tell this, utter it even to the end of the earth; say ye, The LORD hath redeemed his servant Jacob.'
>
> Isaiah, ch. 48, v. 20

From this passage we see that, at this time, Israel will already have become reconciled to the Lord and come back to the laws of righteousness, and is beginning to be gathered into one people and to go into the 'chambers'. These passages are addressed to all Israel, even to those Israelites who are scattered in all nations, the remnant scattered abroad.

> 'Remove out of the midst of Babylon, and go forth out of the land of the Chaldeans, . . .'
>
> Jeremiah, ch. 50, v. 8
>
> 'For Israel hath not been forsaken, nor Judah of his God, of the LORD of hosts; though their land was filled with sin against the Holy One of Israel.'
>
> Jeremiah, ch. 51, v. 5

What a wonderful statement this is. Judah sinned against the Lord Jesus Christ in her rejection of Him, and has continued to do so for nearly two thousand years; yet, here is the statement that implies God's forgiveness! The passage goes on:

> 'Flee out of the midst of Babylon, and deliver every man his soul: be not cut off in her iniquity; for this is the time of the LORD's vengeance; he will render unto her a recompence.'
>
> Jeremiah, ch. 51, v. 6

Now we turn to the book of Revelation:

THE BOAST OF BABYLON – MOTHER AND DAUGHTER

> 'And there followed another angel, saying, Babylon is fallen, is fallen, that great city, because she made all nations drink of the wine of the wrath of her fornication.'
>
> Revelation, ch. 14, v. 8

In war a city is said to have fallen when it is taken over completely by enemy troops, and is totally occupied by the enemy. So in this case Babylon falls into the hands of Satan, utterly and completely, as it is recorded:

> 'And after these things I saw another angel come down from heaven, having great power; and the earth was lightened with his glory. And he cried mightily with a strong voice, saying, Babylon the great is fallen, is fallen, and is become the habitation of devils, and the hold of every foul spirit, and a cage of every unclean and hateful bird. For all nations have drunk of the wine of the wrath of her fornication, and the kings of the earth have committed fornication with her, and the merchants of the earth are waxed rich through the abundance of her delicacies. And I heard another voice from heaven, saying, Come out of her, my people, that ye be not partakers of her sins, and that ye receive not of her plagues.'
>
> Revelation, ch. 18, vs 1–4

This chapter is remarkable for it repeats the boast of Babylon that we saw in Isaiah (ch. 47), thus confirming the timing of the fulfilment of the passage:

> 'How much she hath glorified herself, and lived deliciously, so much torment and sorrow give her: for she saith in her heart, I sit a queen, and am no widow, and shall see no sorrow. Therefore shall her plagues come in one day, death, and mourning, and famine; and she shall be utterly burned with fire: for strong is the Lord God who judgeth her.'
>
> Revelation, ch. 18, vs 7–8

Chapter 4

THE RULE OF THE BEAST

EVERY communistic system has a dictator, and the final 'beast' system will be no exception. Therefore we have to look for the last dictator of the ages who will be in charge when the Lord returns. When this system is set up, it will be the most evil one of all the ages. There will only be two classes of people in it; the ruling class who will be the accepted members of the party, and all others, who will be slaves. Every nation in the group will have a government that will be only administrative, taking its instructions from an overruling council who in turn will take orders from the supreme council acting under the orders of the dictator, who rules over all. This dictator will have the same power as Nebuchadnezzar, of whom it is written, 'Whom he would he slew; and whom he would he kept alive; and whom he would he set up; and whom he would he put down.' (Daniel, ch. 5, v. 19).

It seems that this man must now be alive; for the time remaining would not allow him to be born and to grow up. However, he is not yet revealed, and so we do not know who he is. We can only imagine the terrible condition of the people, and how vile this man will be, and even then we will find that it beggars our imagination. Let us thank the Lord that such a horror is hidden from our eyes until the eve of its formation. We can get some idea of the life in that state by reading what the Bible has to say in Revelation (ch. 18, v. 2). There we read, 'Babylon the great is fallen', but this does not mean that it has come to an end. A state falls when it becomes completely subdued by the enemy and is absolutely under its control, and this final state will be completely under the rule of the evil

THE RULE OF THE BEAST

forces, acting under the man whom Satan has chosen and fully controls. Thus:

> 'Babylon the great is fallen, is fallen, and is become the habitation of devils, and the hold of every foul spirit, . . .'
>
> Revelation, ch. 18, v. 2

We believe that when Satan rebelled against the Lord God Almighty in heaven, one-third of the angels followed him. These were divided into two divisions, devils and evil spirits. The most powerful and evil of them were enclosed in the bottomless pit before mankind came on the earth. Now they must be released so that the destruction of all evil may be accomplished, and so we read:

> 'And the fifth angel sounded, and I saw a star fall from heaven unto the earth: and to him was given the key of the bottomless pit. And he opened the bottomless pit . . .'
>
> Revelation, ch. 9, vs 1–2

The chapter then proceeds to tell us about the evil angels who were imprisoned there. They are ordered to the earth's surface, but they are forbidden to hurt 'the grass of the earth, neither any green thing, neither any tree' (v. 4). They are only allowed to hurt those who have not the seal of God in their foreheads. They are forbidden to kill anyone, but may hurt them with terrible pain, like the pain from the sting of a scorpion, a pain so acute that 'in those days shall men seek death, and shall not find it; and shall desire to die, and death shall flee from them.' (v. 6).

These, the worst of the angels of the rebellion, are under a leader who is named in verse eleven: 'And they had a king over them, which is the angel of the bottomless pit, whose name in the Hebrew tongue is Abaddon, but in the Greek tongue hath his name Apollyon.' This means 'the destroyer' in both tongues. This is the leader who destroys Christianity in the Gentile world. He it is who makes war on the two witnesses, and who kills them in the streets of Babylon, when they have completed their God-given commission to preach to the Gentile world, Christ, and him crucified for the sins of the world. Thus, the day of grace ends, and the day of judgment begins. These evil spirits are responsible for the intense hatred against all Christians throughout the world and, therefore, against Israel.

Satan has had the leadership of all the evil forces which have been operating on the earth against mankind since Adam fell as his first victim. We know something of what devil-possession means, sometimes madness in some form or other; at other times either coldblooded desire to hurt and see people suffer, or to kill. Satan also has the power of the air (Ephesians, ch. 2, v. 2).

Before we can describe the state of the nations, we must first see the kind of man that will be their overlord. He must be Satan-possessed and evil personified. At present we are not quite near enough to the Coming of the Lord to see and name this man. Nevertheless, we can get an impression of what he will be, and what he will be like, so that we shall recognise him when he appears on the scene. I feel sure the man now exists, for it seems very unreasonable to believe that he is not yet born.

God in His foreknowledge saw every one of us before the world was created and knew everything we would do, and every influence that would direct our daily lives. God also foresaw our attitude to all these matters, so we are not controlled by fate to do things. God is not a dictator. He did not totally shape our course for us, but He left us with a will of our own, to make decisions which shape our destiny. However, He also foresaw the decisions we would make if we would let Him guide us. He knew the very moment when He could step into our lives and still leave us freedom of action to shape our lives to meet our eternal existence.

God did not force Judas to obey His will to betray our Lord, but He knew how Judas would react to the temptation of

Satan, to make him take the action he did. If Judas could have seen the result of such action he would have been horrified. So in our freedom of will we are led by Satan to commit sin, but when we turn to the Lord He forgives, and frees us from all sin, and so leaves us free from the result of such sinful actions; but He had to pay the price of that sin before it could be annulled.

God foresaw that a man would be born who would love power and be ruthless in obtaining it, the same as He sees man with a love of money, stooping to every form of greed, in his attempt to obtain it. So this final, and most evil man which the world has ever known, or will ever know, was foreseen by God, and so God will use him and his wickedness to bring about the ensured peace of the world for ever and ever. This will mean the removal of all evil influences, making it impossible for Satan to guide men into evil.

Can we really estimate what the final state of the nations will be like, when the whole Gentile world will be possessed by demons? We can see something of their plight by turning to Jeremiah chapter twenty-five:

> 'Then took I the cup at the LORD's hand, and made all the nations to drink, (v. 17) . . . And they shall drink, and be moved (shaken), and be mad, (v. 16) . . . And it shall be, if they refuse to take the cup at thine hand to drink, then shalt thou say unto them, Thus saith the LORD of hosts; Ye shall certainly drink. (v. 28) . . . Therefore thou shalt say unto them, Thus saith the LORD of hosts, the God of Israel; Drink ye, and be drunken, and spue, and fall, and rise no more, because of the sword which I will send among you. (v. 27)'

The time factor is given in verse 29. 'For, lo, I begin to bring evil on the city which is called by my name.' We are beginning to see many nations forming up against the Israelis, including even those who were once helping them, like France. This is because the Arab world is using the oil which we found and developed for them, as a weapon and as a means of blackmail. They are making the nations pay high prices for it, and besides this are making conditions about the help that they may give to the Israelis. All this shows how near we are getting to the end time.

It is impossible to even attempt to describe the miserable condition of the inhabitants of the Gentile world, when all the evil spirits are in their midst, and are enclosed there by the Lord, so that the iron curtain is tightly drawn round them to keep the evil spirits in.

Before we probe deeper into this terrible state of affairs, and realise that the hatred of Satan's hosts will be against the Israel block of nations, we must ask ourselves – What defence have we in that day? We find the answer in Daniel:

> 'And at that time shall Michael stand up, the great prince which standeth for the children of thy people: and there shall be a time of trouble, such as never was since there was a nation even to that same time.'
>
> Daniel, ch. 12, v. 1

We are sure of a great defence (see ch. 2), so that the people of God will be kept quite safe from the infiltration of the evil forces, and so now we can go on to see something of the personality of this terrible Satan-possessed fiend. He is described in several places in the Word of God. For example:

> 'Behold, his soul which is lifted up is not upright in him: but the just shall live by his (own) faith. Yea also, because he transgresseth by wine, he is a proud man, neither keepeth at home, who enlargeth his desire as hell, and is as death, and cannot be satisfied, but gathereth unto him all nations, and heapeth unto him all people.'
>
> Habakkuk, ch. 2, vs 4–5

Here, we see the man of evil. He starts off slowly but gets more and more evil, following the usual course of all dictators such as Hitler and Stalin. However, this man is being used by God for the final strife of the ages, and as a result of his greed and his activities he has a complete eclipse, and in verse 14 we read:

> 'For the earth shall be filled with the knowledge of the glory of the LORD, as the waters cover the sea.'

The beauty of this verse lies in the fact that all people under the communist regime will have been brain-washed and believe just what the leaders want them to believe, but when the Lord comes they are freed from this tyranny, and learn the knowledge of the glory of God, and find the knowledge of the one true and living God and His love and righteousness, and live in the peace of God, a peace such as they have never had.

In Daniel this man is called 'the king of the north':

> 'And the king shall do according to his will; and he shall exalt himself, and magnify himself above every god, and shall speak marvellous things against the God of gods, and shall prosper till the indignations be accomplished: for that that is determined shall be done.'
>
> Daniel, ch. 11, v. 36

This describes communism, which teaches that there is no God, and therefore, that the leader of the system is the supreme person of the human race who are the supreme beings of all life, and that there is no spiritual life, so that this man is supreme over all life. He can only magnify himself or enlarge his own image by making the image of God smaller than his own. This can only be done by making the Almighty God a myth. (Stalin tried to do this by keeping villages in different parts of Russia short of food. The teachers in the schools set the children praying to God for three days to send them something to eat, then the teachers told them that God did not answer, so now they must pray to Stalin to see if he could hear and answer their prayers. All day they prayed to Stalin and the next day lorries of food came pouring in for the people.) We are also told in this verse that, once he is in power, he will stay there until 'the indignation be accomplished', so he will be a strong leader until the Coming of the Lord.

> 'Neither shall he regard the God of his fathers, nor the desire of women, nor regard any god: for he shall magnify himself above all.'
>
> Daniel, ch. 11, v. 37

In Isaiah we read that he would call himself the 'I am', the name that the Lord called Himself when He formed Israel into a nation. This man will also despise women as something inferior to men.

> 'But in his estate shall he honour the God of forces . . .'
> Daniel, ch. 11, v. 38

Not only will he present himself as 'God' but he will confer on the armed forces, which he will place over the people, the power of godhead inferior only to himself. This makes a second god. Now for the trinity of godhead. He will not stop here, but he will go on with Satan, playing his devilish game, bringing a trinity of gods against the Holy Trinity of the true Godhead:

> '. . . and a god whom his fathers knew not shall he honour with gold, and silver, and with precious stones, and pleasant things.'
> Daniel, ch. 11, v. 38

Everything to make this god look attractive to the people!

> 'Thus shall he do in the most strong holds with a strange god, whom he shall acknowledge and increase with glory: and he shall cause them to rule over many, and shall divide the land for gain.'
> Daniel, ch. 11, v. 39

Notice that this god is an idol decked with jewels. The idol is first made, and so it is in the singular, but later it is found in every stronghold throughout the land over which the dictator rules.

We now leave this chapter till a later study and take up the explanation of the idol in Revelation chapter thirteen, remembering that it is an idol such as never was before. All the past religious cults had idols; all pointed to things that were supposed to give rewards if worshipped, the sun, moon, stars, etc. Always the priests made idols to give them power over the people. Set the people worshipping before them, and in a few generations the people would begin to look like the idol, and conform to what was portrayed in the idol. The Roman Church

THE RULE OF THE BEAST

has an image too, a mother with a little babe in her arms trusting its mother, and so she calls herself the Mother Church, and expects all her adherents to trust her in whatever she teaches. Babylon in its day made an image of gold and set the people worshipping it, and the world has been prostrate at its feet ever since, a metal that is too soft for anything except to adorn oneself.

In Revelation we see the rule of the beast, a study that occupies much of this chapter:

> '. . . and they worshipped the beast, saying, Who is like unto the beast? who is able to make war with him? And there was given unto him a mouth speaking great things and blasphemies; and power was given unto him to continue forty and two months. And he opened his mouth in blasphemy against God, to blaspheme his name, and his tabernacle, and them that dwell in heaven.'
> Revelation, ch. 13, vs 4–6

The nations are already saying this today even though Russia has not yet come to the zenith of her power. In verse twelve we discover a description of the beast which links up with that given in Daniel chapter eleven.

> 'And he exerciseth all the power of the first beast before him, and causeth the earth and them which dwell therein to worship the first beast, whose deadly wound was healed. And he doeth great wonders, so that he maketh fire come down from heaven on the earth in the sight of men, And deceiveth them that dwell on the earth by the means of those miracles which he had power to do in the sight of the beast; saying to them that dwell on the earth, that they should make an image to the beast, which had the wound by a sword, and did live.'
> Revelation, ch. 13, vs 12–14

So here we have the image of Daniel chapter two. It is the image of the beast system, into which is placed all the teaching of the system.

> 'And he had power to give life unto the image of the beast, that the image of the beast should both speak, and cause that as many as would not worship the image of the beast should be killed.'
> Revelation, ch. 13, v. 15

In these days of advanced technology, it is not hard to imagine just what the idol might be like, and why it could be so different from every idol preceeding it. Perhaps a great robot of some kind that is drawn into the market place of the cities, and, all the people being ordered to appear before it, the electric current is turned on and a wave of vibrations broadcasting the beliefs of communism flows closely over the heads of all the people. Any person who even thinks anything contrary to these vibrations will be detected and identified. The victims will then be brought out before the idol which will ask them questions, maybe from a tape machine. There could be a sophisticated lie detector so that if any person even thinks, "No, I don't accept it" while he is saying "Yes", then that person will be automatically executed. I know this sounds fantastic today, but tomorrow it may be proved all too possible. We know that with the aid of wires fixed to the head, the waves of the brain can be measured, so there is not much more to be done to make such an image workable.

We can only pray for those who may have to face such a situation and daily praise and thank the Lord that, when it does become part of the machinery for enslaving the people of the communist world (so that they will be afraid even to think in case a thought leads to death), we will be kept safe by the Lord our God. Yes; safe in the Chambers mentioned in Isaiah. After we have tried to bring peace to the world and completely failed; and after we have turned to the Lord and confessed that we have been a failure, the Lord will say to us:

> 'Come, my people, enter thou into thy chambers, and shut thy doors about thee: hide thyself as it were for a little moment, until the indignation be overpast. For, behold, the LORD cometh out of his place to punish the inhabitants of the earth for their iniquity . . .'
>
> Isaiah, ch. 26, vs 20–21

Chapter 5

ECONOMIC JUDGMENT ON THE NATIONS AND THE MARK OF THE BEAST

WE HAVE already seen the explanation of the four horses of Revelation chapter six. In this chapter we are going to study the third horse:

> 'And when he had opened the third seal, I heard the third beast say, Come and see. And I beheld, and lo a black horse; and he that sat on him had a pair of balances in his hand. And I heard a voice in the midst of the four beasts say, A measure of wheat for a penny, and three measures of barley for a penny; and see thou hurt not the oil and the wine.'
>
> Revelation, ch. 6, vs 5–6

The four beasts are representative of Israel, while the four and twenty elders represent the Church (Revelation, ch. 5, v. 14); so here we have a national and an international command from heaven. The rider with his balances is given control of the economic life of the nations. The four beasts tell him that he must not hurt the oil and the wine which are the symbols of the national and spiritual life of Israel in the Islands. However, this command does not cover the state of Israel, which is represented as the branches cut off from the olive tree (Romans, ch. 11, v. 17). It must be remembered that the last three horses with their riders, that roam throughout the world, are all destructive. We are now seeing this black horse in action and the nations worrying over the price and supply of basic commodities – eggs, butter, meat, sugar, etc., and the situation looks like getting worse.

At the present time we are suffering like all the other nations, but that is because of the sins of our nation which have brought about 'Jacob's trouble'. We have mixed with the Gentile nations in the Babylonian system, and now we are paying the price. We are also in that part of the trouble when money, and the love of it (which is the root of all evil) has become a god, and everyone seems to be wanting more and more. Some men are becoming wealthy overnight, and the system is getting out of hand. The exploiters who become millionaires overnight by negotiating land deals and forcing up the price of houses will soon have to pay a heavy price for their greed.

> 'Go to now, ye rich men, weep and howl for your miseries that shall come upon you.'
>
> James, ch. 5, v. 1

When riches are made regardless of the misery brought upon others, those becoming wealthy must suffer themselves. Not all riches are condemned here. Riches are a blessing if they are come by rightly and are used wisely so that others benefit. Riches are not evil, but poverty is a national evil. Deuteronomy, ch. 15, vs 4–5:

> 'Save when there shall be no poor among you; for the LORD shall greatly bless thee in the land which the LORD thy God giveth thee for an inheritance to possess it: Only if thou carefully hearken unto the voice of the LORD thy God, to observe to do all these commandments which I command thee this day.'

The Lord condemned the Jews for not keeping the Law when He said '. . . ye have the poor always with you' (Matthew, ch. 26, v. 11). The Lord tells us that we shall be saved out of Jacob's trouble, and then, our economy will be put to right. The Law will be to the effect that all must live except the slackers:

> '. . . if any would not work, neither should he eat.'
>
> II Thessalonians, ch. 3, v. 10

If the Law were to be put into effect now, it would correct a national scandal. If a man cannot work that is a different matter. He should be provided for.

When we come out of the Babylonian system and come into our Chambers, then we will leave Babylon to experience the economic crash which will follow. This is the prophecy of Revelation, chapter 18, vs 10–11:

ECONOMIC JUDGMENT

> '. . . Alas, alas, that great city Babylon, that mighty city! for in one hour is thy judgment come. And the merchants of the earth shall weep and mourn over her; for no man buyeth their merchandise any more.'

There will then follow a great trade recession. First, all the luxury trades go bankrupt – merchandise of gold, silver and precious stones and of pearls. Then the sale of fine cloth and silks will fail. Then precious wood, brass, iron and marble become unsaleable, followed by the spices and scents. The downward trend continues to include trade in wine, oil, flour, wheat and meat, transport and dismissal of servants, and finally the souls of men.

> 'And the fruits that thy soul lusted after are departed from thee, and all things which were dainty and goodly are departed from thee, and thou shalt find them no more at all. The merchants of these things, which were made rich by her, shall stand afar off for the fear of her torment, weeping and wailing.'
>
> Revelation, ch. 18, vs 14–15

It naturally follows that when trade dries up, the world's sea trade must be affected:

> '. . . And every shipmaster, and all the company in ships, and sailors, and as many as trade by sea, stood afar off, And cried when they saw the smoke of her burning. . . . Alas, alas, that great city, wherein were made rich all that had ships in the sea by reason of her costliness! for in one hour is she made desolate.'
>
> Revelation, ch. 18, vs 17–19

That this takes place at the end of the age, as part of the 'terrible day of the Lord', is made plain in verse twenty. It is a great judgment by the Lord God Almighty. The collapse is so great that we read that all entertainment will cease, and that all craftsmen of all trades will find no work. Even the grinding of the corn will be no more. Thus the judgment is complete.

The Lord said, 'Vengeance is mine; I will repay' (Romans, ch. 12, v. 19) and the time has come when the Lord is beginning to reap the harvest of evil in the world.

> 'Rejoice over her, thou heaven, and ye holy apostles and prophets; for God hath avenged you on her. And a mighty angel took up a stone like

a great millstone, and cast it into the sea, saying, Thus with violence shall that great city Babylon be thrown down, and shall be found no more at all . . . And in her was found the blood of prophets, and of saints, and of all that were slain upon the earth.'
Revelation, ch. 18, vs 20, 21 and 24

The judgments are not completed at this stage, but all the slain in all the wars that were caused by men like Hitler are included in this verse. Notice there is no word about the great battle of the terrible day of the Lord in this chapter. In fact, chapter fifteen, chapter sixteen and chapter seventeen (which deals with the fall of Rome and the final establishment of the Babylonian system under Russia) do not refer to the great battle. This great battle is the subject of chapter nineteen. There are some events which we have yet to see before it can occur.

We must deal now with the period when Israel has been drawn into her Chambers; the day of grace has come to an end; and the judgments of the Lord are in the earth. The division is given in chapter thirteen. On the one hand there will be all who have received the signs of slavery in the communistic world (these are given in Revelation chapter thirteen),

'. . . that no man might buy or sell, save he that had the mark, or the name of the beast, or the number of his name.'
Revelation, ch. 13, v. 17

'. . . If any man worship the beast and his image, and receive his mark in his forehead, or in his hand, The same shall drink of the wine of the wrath of God . . .'
Revelation, ch. 14, vs 9–10

'And it was given unto him (the beast) to make war with the saints, and to overcome them: and power was given him over all kindreds, and tongues, and nations. And all that dwell upon the earth shall worship him, whose names are not written in the book of life of the Lamb slain from the foundation of the world.'
Revelation, ch. 13, vs 7–8

On the other hand there will be the saints. Here then are the two sides of this world-wide division. The saints are safe because they have their names in the book of life, and it behoves us all to make sure that we are in this number, and not with those

ECONOMIC JUDGMENT

that have the mark and name of the beast. Once this division has taken place there can be no soul saved, because the Holy Spirit will no longer lead people to the Lord, as it is written:

> 'And he saith unto me, Seal not the sayings of the prophecy of this book: for the time is at hand. He that is unjust, let him be unjust still: and he which is filthy, let him be filthy still: and he that is righteous, let him be righteous still: and he that is holy, let him be holy still.'
> Revelation, ch. 22, vs 10–11

As one will be unable to buy or sell without 'the mark' of the beast, it would seem as though this is an international monetary system for all the Babylonian nations, and unless a nation is willing to adopt this system, there will be no trading between them and the Communist-Babylonian countries. The German monetary unit is called the Mark, and the unit currency in the Common Market will be the Com-Mark, and so it seems possible that the Bible is more accurate than I can explain, for 'the mark' is both in their hands and on their foreheads. (Revelation, ch. 13, v. 16).

When Cain killed his brother Abel, he did it in a moment of anger. The Bible Law says that a man must receive the death penalty if a murder was done in cold blood and was a premeditated act. Cain's slaying of his brother was not so, and therefore the penalty was not death but exile, and the mark that the Lord placed upon him was for his own protection (Genesis, ch. 15, v. 15). The same rule applies in Ezekiel, where the Lord ordered that all the sinners be slain.

> 'And he called to the man clothed with linen, which had the writer's inkhorn by his side; And the LORD said unto him, Go through the midst of the city, through the midst of Jerusalem, and set a mark upon the foreheads of the men that sigh and that cry for all the abominations that be done in the midst thereof. And to the others he said in mine hearing, Go ye after him through the city, and smite: let not your eye spare, neither have ye pity: Slay utterly old and young, both maids, and little children, and women: but come not near any man upon whom is the mark . . .'
> Ezekiel, ch. 9, vs 3–6

We see the same action involving the one hundred and forty and four thousand recorded in Revelation:

> 'And I saw another angel ascending from the east, having the seal of the living God: and he cried with a loud voice to the four angels, to whom it was given to hurt the earth and the sea, Saying, Hurt not the earth, neither the sea, nor the trees, till we have sealed the servants of our God in their foreheads.'
>
> Revelation, ch. 7, vs 2–3

Here again the mark of the Lord is for their protection. It will keep them safe in the same way that the blood upon the doorposts and lintels of the houses of Israel meant protection when the angel of death went to every house in Egypt. There the Lord promised to those who stayed indoors, sheltered by the blood, that 'the LORD will pass over the door, and will not suffer the destroyer to come unto your houses to smite you' (Exodus, ch. 12, v. 23).

When we turn to the graded rewards to the saints in the messages to the seven Churches in Asia, we find that to some will be given a white stone with a name upon it; to others will be given the morning star; and apparently the highest reward will be:

> 'Him that overcometh will I make a pillar in the temple of my God, and he shall go no more out: and I will write upon him the name of my God, and the name of the city of my God, which is new Jerusalem, which cometh down out of heaven from my God: and I will write upon him my new name.'
>
> Revelation, ch. 3, v. 12

These are all awards to the faithful for their faithfulness. We will have to wait and see if these are some kind of visible decorations, or whether they are invisible, but symbolise a high position. I cannot tell what it will be or how it will be done; only time will show us what the Bible means.

The number 666 is certainly important, but again, I for one cannot tell how it will be finally applied, and it would be wrong to try and guess. Those who study Bible numbers, point out that all evil men in the past have had this number in some form or another.

We know that in the communist system there are two classes

of people, those in the party and those who are not. Perhaps these signs will show which class a person is in, in the last communist state. We do know that the mark of the beast and the number 666 will decide the degree of slavery of the people, and that possessing these marks will bring them into condemnation by the Lord. We know that they cannot reign with Christ for the thousand years (see Revelation, ch. 20, v. 4). We also know that those who have these marks will suffer from the wrath of God:

> 'And the third angel followed them, saying with a loud voice, If any man worship the beast and his image, and receive his mark in his forehead, or in his hand, The same shall drink of the wine of the wrath of God, which is poured out without mixture into the cup of his indignation . . .'
>
> Revelation, ch. 14, vs 9–10

Thus, the world will be divided into two parts. First, those who have all the marks of evil and are in the outside world and second, those unmarked by evil living in the Chambers who are in the safe keeping of the Lord. The members of the Church in the outside world will suffer at the hands of the rulers of the evil states, while many in Israel who have sold their souls to Satan, by adopting communism or some heathen form of worship, will receive the marks of condemnation together with the rest of the world.

The Israel block of nations will be safe, for the Lord will divide the nations. All the Israel stock who have not accepted communism or other heathen practices, will be brought into the Chambers of safety:

> 'Fear not: for I am with thee: I will bring thy seed from the east, and gather thee from the west; I will say to the north, Give up; and to the south, Keep not back: bring my sons from far, and my daughters from the ends of the earth; Even every one that is called by my name: for I have created him for my glory, I have formed him; yea, I have made him.'
>
> Isaiah, ch. 43, vs 5–7

If all the Israel stock is to be gathered out of the Gentile world before it goes into absolute evil, then there must be a place for the ingathering of Israel. This place cannot be Palestine because it is reserved as the site of the great battle at the end of the age.

First there is the command of the Lord that Israelites will have to obey, 'I will bring thy seed from the east, and gather thee from the west; I will say to the north, Give up; and to the south, Keep not back:'. This means they will be forced out of non-Israelite lands. With leaders like General Amin one can see this happening. Such evil men do not know it, but they are doing the work of the Lord in driving His people to their places of safety. These places of safety are mentioned in Isaiah, ch. 26, vs 20–21:

> 'Come, my people, enter thou into thy chambers, and shut thy doors about thee: hide thyself as it were for a little moment, until the indignation be overpast. For, behold, the LORD cometh out of his place to punish the inhabitants of the earth for their iniquity . . .'

The command to make our exodus is also given in Revelation, ch. 18, vs 4–5:

> 'And I heard another voice from heaven, saying, Come out of her, my people, that ye be not partakers of her sins, and that ye receive not of her plagues. For her sins have reached unto heaven, and God hath remembered her iniquities.'

The plagues will cover the whole of the Gentile world, but before we can enter into our Chambers we will have to fight off a communist attack which is now close at hand. It will not be easy, but the experience will lead us to turn to the Lord God of Israel. Already the Throne is being attacked and Parliament is being defied by certain communist trade union leaders. We know the Lord will give us the victory in the end and we will find our God!

Chapter 6

THE PLAGUES (PART 1)

IN THE last chapter we saw the complete breakdown of the communist economic system which follows the takeover by Russia of the whole of Europe. This is the natural result of total nationalisation of all industry and commerce. After this nationalisation, all incentive and initiative of the individual to improve his position and invent things for his own advantage, and for the good of others, will be a crime against the state. He must be satisfied with whatever status it has pleased his overlords to appoint to him. If, however, he is an active member of the party he will be promoted (but not otherwise). The workers will be just like ants, all working for the community, with no hope of anything for themselves. Under these conditions economic collapse must follow and misery for the people because the state will be held together only by the iron hand of the state police. So much is common sense, and involves the natural laws of cause and effect.

The plagues are entirely different, they are supernatural direct acts of the Lord God Almighty.

When mankind came first on the earth, the Lord kept all evil under control by the forces of nature – the waters of the flood, confusion of tongues, fire, famines, storms, sickness, etc. – all these are elements of nature. In fact when natural disasters happen today they are still called 'acts of God'.

When the Lord separated Israel from the Gentile nations, and brought them into the Kingdom of God on earth, He appointed them to keep the nations under control by maintaining a powerful position in the earth. So we read:

'The portion of Jacob is not like them; for he is the former of all things: and Israel is the rod of his inheritance: the LORD of hosts (battles) is his name. Thou art my battle axe and weapons of war: . . . with thee will I destroy kingdoms.'

Jeremiah, ch. 51, vs 19–20

When we had a great navy we commanded the peace of the seas and ended slavery. Had we been true to the Lord and acted as keepers of the peace, and ordered the nations to keep from evil, with strong armed forces to command the nations to keep from worldly ambitions, we could have held the peace of the world. Sadly we were not willing to keep strong fighting forces because of the heavy cost, and so, motivated by Satan, warlike nations saw our weakness and struck out for world domination. Consequently, Israel had to fight two World Wars in one generation before we broke them in pieces. Today we are making the same grave error. We are reducing the size of our army, navy, and air force, while Russia and her allies are arming with all their might.

Twice before we have paid a heavy price for our folly and in the natural course of events we would have to pay again in a third world war. However, this time the Lord will intervene and we will cease to be God's battle axe and will be enclosed in our Chambers. The moment this happens our fighting days will be over. We will enter the Chambers as a weak fighting force but, while we are there, we will become 'a kingdom of priests, and an holy nation' (Exodus, ch. 19, v. 6). The priesthood of Israel never fought in a battle. So at this time the Lord will not use Israel to counter the evil forces of the world, but will return to using the elements of nature as His weapons.

Consequently we have to study the six plagues that will take place before the great battle of the Lord God Almighty.

In referring to the events of the near future in relationship to Israel's role, the Bible often links them to the release from bondage which occurred when Israel came out of Egypt. At that time the Lord used ten plagues to break the power of Egypt. In

THE PLAGUES (PART 1)

Revelation chapter sixteen, and in chapters eight and nine, seven future plagues are mentioned.

In Egypt the initial sign of God's power to free Israel was limited to Pharaoh's house. Moses and Aaron went to Pharaoh, and Aaron cast down his rod and it became a serpent and the wise men of Pharaoh's court did likewise.

In the first plague, the Lord turned all the rivers and streams of Egypt into blood. The second plague was that of frogs which entered all the houses. The third was that of lice, and it was at this point that the Lord separated the Israelites from the Egyptians.

Pharaoh had ordered the Israelites to go all over Egypt collecting straw to make bricks (see Exodus, ch. 5, vs 6–12). Yet we read in Exodus chapter eight (vs 22–23):

> 'And I will sever in that day the land of Goshen, in which my people dwell, that no swarms of flies shall be there; to the end thou mayest know that I am the LORD in the midst of the earth. And I will put a division between my people and thy people: to morrow shall this sign be.'

The next day the Lord brought all the people of Israel into the land of Goshen and all the taskmasters in Egypt could not hold the slaves because God gave them freedom in a land of safety while the remaining six plagues fell on the rest of the land of Egypt. This means that the plagues were geographically limited. The people in Egypt suffered, except those in Goshen who did not.

In the same way we will be in our Chambers while the six plagues of Revelation chapter sixteen fall on our enemies. We will be looking on, beholding the works of the Lord. Any Israelite not in the Chambers will suffer, but any stranger who is in the Chambers will not.

We have already seen that Satan's attempt to capture Israel by a great wave of communism fails, and so we read:

> 'And the dragon was wroth with the woman, and went to make war with the remnant of her seed, which keep the commandments of God, and have the testimony of Jesus Christ.'
>
> Revelation, ch. 12, v. 17

We know that this 'remnant' does not refer to the Jews who refuse to believe in Jesus, but it will apply to the northern house of Israel after their awakening and re-entry into their Chambers.

Soon all the armies of Europe will be under the control of the Russian dictator and will be massed on the other side of the Channel, while Britain will be looking to the Lord for her defence. Knowledge of this situation reveals the meaning of the first three plagues. In Ezekiel the Lord says:

> '... Thus saith the Lord GOD; Behold, I am against thee, O Gog, the chief prince of Meshech and Tubal: And I will turn thee back, and put hooks into thy jaws ...'
>
> Ezekiel, ch. 38, vs 3–4

So the question is, "How does the Lord keep the armies from crossing the water?" Remember, planes and bombs can destroy a land, but to capture it and to subdue its people, there must be an invading army of infantry. Satan's objective is to take over Israel and rule over it through Russia; God's plan is to keep Israel free. The first three plagues are for the defence of Israel. The first plague is described in Revelation chapter sixteen verses one and two:

> 'And I heard a great voice out of the temple saying to the seven angels, Go your ways, and pour out the vials of the wrath of God upon the earth. And the first went, and poured out his vial upon the earth; and there fell a noisome and grievous sore (Greek – evil and painful) upon the men which had the mark of the beast, and upon them which worshipped his image.'

This plague will affect the whole armed forces of Russia and her European allies on land, sea and in the air, and will bring all movement to a halt, for men suffering like this cannot fight as long as the sores remain.

THE PLAGUES (PART 1)

How long they will last we cannot tell: all we know is that the time will be useful to the Israel block of nations as they unite to form a single front against the enemy. Thus will they fulfil again the parable of Ezekiel:

> 'Moreover, thou son of man, take thee one stick, and write upon it, For Judah, and for the children of Israel his companions: then take another stick, and write upon it, For Joseph, the stick of Ephraim, and for all the house of Israel: his companions. . . . Thus saith the Lord GOD; Behold, I will take the stick of Joseph, which is in the hand of Ephraim, and the tribes of Israel his fellows, and will put them with him, even with the stick of Judah, and make them one stick, and they shall be one in mine hand.'
> Ezekiel, ch. 37, vs 16 and 19

This passage embraces all Israel. Notice the 'companions' have become 'tribes', and they are his fellows. Thus we will see the various parts of Israel, in the British Isles and Ireland, in Canada and the U.S.A., in southern Africa, and in Australia and New Zealand, every one of them in direct danger from the communists, all joining with each other under the Throne of David (which is in the midst of Ephraim) to meet the common danger and complete isolation from the rest of the world. Even now, as communism (with China at its head) is gaining control over the Far East, Australia is speaking about enlarging her armed forces to meet the danger of invasion. South Africa and Rhodesia are in danger from a united black Africa. America is in danger from communism in Central and South America. The danger will look formidable with the Russian navies in all seas, including nuclear submarines which are able to be very destructive. The nations of Israel will be able to close their doors. How they will do it is not quite clear but the defences will be the Lord's, so we know it will be effective and we will be safe. Israel has never been told to defend land frontiers. This is the mistake that the U.S.A. made in the Far East, with terrible losses in men, money and prestige in Vietnam. It is also the mistake we are making by keeping our forces in West Germany. We are plainly told that our defence line is the sea. The Lord told Abraham that He would give to his seed 'the gate' of their enemies. Thus we have the seas as a natural defence. All the nations of the Israel commonwealth are behind the seas (with the exception of Rhodesia, who instead has three rivers cutting her off from the mainland of Africa). We can shut ourselves off in our own lands, but we will have lost control of the seas, while Russia will have the greatest navy that has ever been known. She will be in sole control of the Mediterranean Sea as the Bible tells. Even now her ships are coming right up to our coasts, spying out our defences. This is the greatest danger of all, for it means that we could be starved into submission, as we nearly were in the last war. We might ask ourselves "What can God do about it?" The answer comes from the Bible, 'Is anything too hard for the LORD?' (Genesis, ch. 18, v. 14). As we know, it is not: so we can put our trust in Him. How much must we suffer for our waywardness (as we did in the last war) before God comes to our aid? The answer is, only until the second plague:

> 'And the second angel poured out his vial upon the sea: and it became as the blood of a dead man: and every living soul died in the sea.'
> Revelation, ch. 16, v. 3

and in Revelation chapter eight (vs 8–9) we read:

> 'And the second angel sounded, and as it were a great mountain burning with fire was cast into the sea; and the third part of the sea became blood; And the third part of the creatures which were in the sea, and had life, died, and the third part of the ships were destroyed.'

Thus, Israel is preserved by God so that there can never be a Russian invasion. This action by God is completed by the third plague of Revelation chapter eight:

> 'And the third angel sounded, and there fell a great star from heaven, burning as it were a lamp, and it fell upon the third part of the rivers, and upon the fountains of waters; And the name of the star is called Wormwood (Hebrew – undrinkable): and the third part of the waters became wormwood; and many men died of the waters, because they were made bitter.'
> Revelation, ch. 8, vs 10–11

THE PLAGUES (PART 1)

These plagues also affect the East for we read (Revelation, ch. 9, vs 13–14):

> 'And the sixth angel sounded, and I heard a voice from the four horns of the golden altar which is before God, Saying to the sixth angel which had the trumpet, Loose the four angels which are bound in the great river Euphrates.'

Turning back now to Revelation chapter sixteen, verse four, we read:

> 'And the third angel poured out his vial upon the rivers and fountains of waters; and they became blood.'

An invading force must be well supplied with all kinds of materials. So for an invasion of the Israel nations there must be a large fleet of supply ships which are kept in the rivers ready to sail the moment the enemy has command of the sea. Even these supply ships are destroyed by the Lord.

These three plagues make the Israel countries absolutely safe and give back to them the command of the seas, and thereby God keeps His promise by giving Israel 'the gate of his enemies' (Genesis, ch. 22, v. 17).

After the third plague there follows in Revelation chapter sixteen a summary and the verdict of heaven concerning the first three plagues:

> 'And I heard the angel of the waters say, Thou art righteous, O Lord, which art, and wast, and shalt be, because thou hast judged thus. For they have shed the blood of saints and prophets, and thou hast given them blood to drink; for they are worthy. And I heard another out of the altar say, Even so, Lord God Almighty, true and righteous are thy judgments.'
>
> Revelation, ch. 16, vs 5–7

Here is the justice of heaven keeping faith with the saints and the prophets to whom God promised, 'Vengeance is mine; I will repay':

> 'Recompense to no man evil for evil. Provide things honest in the sight of all men. . . . Dearly beloved, avenge not yourselves, but rather give place unto wrath: for it is written, Vengeance is mine; I will repay, saith the Lord. Therefore if thine enemy hunger, feed him; if he thirst,

give him drink: for in so doing thou shalt heap coals of fire on his head. Be not overcome of evil, but overcome evil with good.'
Romans, ch. 12, vs 17 and 19–21

In these plagues we see revealed something of what the vengeance of God can be. So in Hebrews we read:

'For we know him that hath said, Vengeance belongeth unto me, I will recompense, saith the Lord. And again, The Lord shall judge his people. It is a fearful thing to fall into the hands of the living God.'
Hebrews, ch. 10, vs 30–31

At this point it is interesting to go back and consider the time when Israel was freed from the bondage of Egypt.

Moses took Israel towards the Red Sea and so led them into what appeared to be a trap with the sea in front and the armies of Egypt behind. They need not have taken this route to the sea but could have taken a shorter route by land. Pharaoh was also led into the trap prepared by the Lord.

'And it came to pass, when Pharaoh had let the people go, that God led them not through the way of the land of the Philistines, although that was near; for God said, Lest peradventure the people repent when they see war, and they return to Egypt.'
Exodus, ch. 13, v. 17

It often happens that God cuts off our retreat when we would go back to the old paths. According to Pharaoh's reckoning, Moses was in a trap. So he gathered all the chariots of Egypt, and went after them (Exodus, ch. 14, v. 9):

'But the Egyptians pursued after them, all the horses and chariots of Pharaoh, and his horsemen, and his army, . . .'

All this great army went against 600,000 unarmed men with their families. Then the Lord used the sea to preserve Israel and give them complete freedom from the fear of Egypt, and in addition, He destroyed all the army of Egypt in the Red Sea. This is very interesting when we consider the way the Lord will once again preserve His people by destroying the enemy in the sea.

History in God's hands does repeat itself, and God always saves the best and greatest till last!

Chapter 7

THE PLAGUES (PART 2)

> 'And the fourth angel poured out his vial upon the sun; and power was given unto him to scorch men with fire. And men were scorched with great heat, and blasphemed the name of God, which hath power over these plagues: and they repented not to give him glory.'
> Revelation, ch. 16, vs 8 and 9

AGAIN we see the greatness of the Lord. With each plague there is the invitation to acknowledge God and to give glory to Him but instead they blaspheme the name of the Lord.

This is the only plague that falls upon Israel, and even then it is controlled.

> 'And I will send a fire on Magog, and among them that dwell carelessly in the isles: and they shall know that I am the LORD. So will I make my holy name known in the midst of my people Israel; and I will not let them pollute my holy name any more: and the heathen shall know that I am the LORD, the Holy One in Israel.'
> Ezekiel, ch. 39, vs 6–7

This is a plague which makes those living carelessly in 'the isles' turn to the Lord and acknowledge Him as the Lord. We are told by some students of the Bible that this 'fire' refers to a nuclear war between the nations of Israel and Russia. We are forced to rule this interpretation out, firstly because we could not drop nuclear bombs on the whole of the land Magog (Russia), and secondly because if nuclear bombs landed in these Isles there could be no control over them affecting some people and not others. They would destroy one and all, and the Isles would have to be without population for many years afterwards. The one small A-bomb that fell on Hiroshima in Japan had this result. We can rule out any nuclear war before the Coming of the Lord, and although St. Peter tells us of a terrible event which may involve nuclear activity, we know that this event is in the distant future and is the result of God using the elements of nature. Peter is very careful to tell us that a day with the Lord is as a thousand years so that we will know that he is telling us that there is a thousand years between the events he mentions.

> 'But the day of the Lord will come as a thief in the night; in the which the heavens shall pass away with a great noise, and the elements shall melt with fervent heat, . . . Nevertheless we, according to his promise, look for new heavens and a new earth, wherein dwelleth righteousness.'
>
> II Peter, ch. 3, vs 10 and 13

No, we believe the Bible when it says this will be a natural fire caused by scorching heat from the sun.

Now we must consider the fifth plague of Revelation:

> 'And the fifth angel poured out his vial upon the seat of the beast; and his kingdom was full of darkness; and they gnawed (chewed) their tongues for pain, And blasphemed the God of heaven because of their pains and their sores, and repented not of their deeds.'
>
> Revelation, ch. 16, vs 10–11

These sores could well be the same as those mentioned in Revelation chapter nine where we see the bottomless pit opened and Abaddon and his angels come up out of it to inflict much pain on those who do not have the seal of God in their foreheads. The pain is as the sting of a scorpion and is so bad that men will wish to die. This then could be the double witness of the prophecy.

It looks as if the sores continue throughout the remaining plagues and yet the people still remain in a state of rebellion against the Lord God of heaven. It also seems as though the sores fall more on the leaders of State, as this plague falls upon 'the seat of the beast.' This will bring all authority to a halt and so make government hard to carry out.

The sixth plague preceeds the seventh and final plague which is not described in this chapter but which is the great battle of

THE PLAGUES (PART 2)

the Lord which follows. It appears that as the Lord hardened the heart of Pharaoh at the end of Israel's bondage in Egypt, so He will harden the hearts of the people during these plagues, otherwise it is hard to understand why they do not cry out to the Lord for mercy.

> 'And the sixth angel poured out his vial upon the great river Euphrates; and the water thereof was dried up, that the way of the kings of the east might be prepared.'
>
> Revelation, ch. 16, v. 12

This verse introduces two subjects. Firstly it describes action to open up the way for China and the other communist nations in the Far East, as they try to control Palestine before Russia can. Secondly, it tells of the effect upon the river itself. The River Euphrates is a very long river and it once ran through the city of Babylon in the days of the great empires of Babylon and Medo-Persia. However, it has changed its course and now runs several miles to the west with the result that the old city of Babylon has remained a ruin ever since.

The River Nile, the Suez Canal, the River Jordan and the Dead Sea are all affected at the time of the Coming of the Lord, but it would be inappropriate to deal with these facts just here.

The next verse from Revelation chapter sixteen has already been mentioned in chapter one, but it must be repeated here, as we now deal with the last part of the verse:

> 'And I saw three unclean spirits like frogs come out of the mouth of the dragon, and out of the mouth of the beast, and out of the mouth of the false prophet. For they are the spirits of devils, working miracles, which go forth unto the kings of the earth and of the whole world, to gather them to the battle of that great day of God Almighty.'
>
> Revelation, ch. 16, vs 13–14

Who is this false prophet that is the means of bringing all the nations of the earth to this great battle? We know that the battle will take place at Jerusalem, and we have seen that the false prophet is the same person as was spoken of in Revelation chapter thirteen verse eleven:

> 'And I beheld another beast coming up out of the earth; and he had two horns like a lamb, and he spake as a dragon.'

This is the one that brings all the nations of the world against Jerusalem. He is evil but his actions are being used by the Lord. One reason why the nations want to control Palestine, and why Russia and China both want to get there first is quoted in Ezekiel chapter thirty-eight in the challenge that Israel-Britain will be making to Russia.

> 'Sheba, and Dedan, and the merchants of Tarshish with all the young lions thereof, shall say unto thee, Art thou come to take a spoil? hast thou gathered thy company to take a prey? to carry away silver and gold, to take away cattle and goods, to take a great spoil?'
>
> Ezekiel, ch. 38, v. 13

This verse raises two questions. Who are the 'merchants of Tarshish' and 'the young lions thereof', and what is the 'great spoil'? The ships of Tarshish were the merchant ships in the Old Testament and we must quote them here because there is a school of thought which says that they were Gentile ships. I Kings, ch. 10, v. 22:

> 'For the king had at sea a navy of Tharshish with the navy of Hiram: once in three years came the navy of Tharshish, bringing gold, and silver, ivory, and apes, and peacocks.'

I Kings, ch. 22, v. 48:

> 'Jehoshaphat made ships of Tharshish to go to Ophir (a place in south Arabia from whence the products of India were brought to the West) for gold: but they went not; for the ships were broken at Ezion-geber (which is the gulf of the Red Sea).'

> 'Surely the isles shall wait for me, and the ships of Tarshish first, to bring thy sons from far, their silver and their gold with them, unto the name of the LORD thy God, and to the Holy One of Israel, because he hath glorified thee.'
>
> Isaiah, ch. 60, v. 9

Thus the term 'ships of Tarshish' was, and remains, right up to the Coming of the Lord, the Bible name for the navies of Israel. The 'young lions' are the Israel nations that form the English-

THE PLAGUES (PART 2)

speaking nations of today. This means that we will be making a verbal protest to Russia about her invasion of Palestine.

The 'great spoil' must be in Jerusalem and is the wealth of the nations. Jewry has its vast wealth at present in many nations and it has people in high places in those nations. So we can see that they will know when to take their wealth out in time to transfer it to Jerusalem. They will be hoping that Jerusalem will not be destroyed, but the spoil is lost though not to man. In Zephaniah we read:

> 'The great day of the LORD is near, it is near, and hasteth greatly, even the voice of the day of the LORD: the mighty man shall cry there bitterly. That day is a day of wrath, a day of trouble and distress, a day of wasteness and desolation, a day of darkness and gloominess, a day of clouds and thick darkness. A day of the trumpet and alarm against the fenced cities, and against the high towers. And I will bring distress upon men, that they shall walk like blind men, because they have sinned against the LORD: and their blood shall be poured out as dust, and their flesh as the dung. Neither their silver nor their gold shall be able to deliver them in the day of the LORD's wrath; but the whole land shall be devoured by the fire of his jealousy: for he shall make even a speedy riddance of all them that dwell in the land.'
>
> Zephaniah, ch. 1, vs 14–18

Zechariah takes up the same theme:

> 'Behold, the day of the LORD cometh, and thy spoil shall be divided in the midst of thee. For I will gather all nations against Jerusalem to battle; and the city shall be taken, and the houses rifled, and the women ravished; and half of the city shall go forth into captivity . . .'
>
> Zechariah, ch. 14, vs 1–2

So, when half the city is in the hands of the Russians, half of the spoil will be in their hands, but they will not be able to collect it because of the earthquake that follows so swiftly. This spoil will have been collected by Jewry from all the communist nations who do not believe in God, and who will therefore be classed as the heathen (see verse 14):

> 'And Judah also shall fight at Jerusalem; and the wealth of all the heathen round about shall be gathered together, gold, and silver, and apparel, in great abundance.'

This is a plain statement of the facts as they will be in the day of the Lord's judgments. When we think not only of the combined armies of Europe, but also of China and Japan, we begin to realise the enormous hosts that will be around Judah and surrounding Jerusalem.

It must be understood that the Israeli state in its present form is not the object of this prophecy; it is only a provisional nation holding Palestine until the final Judah nation takes over. The last time Judah fought at Jerusalem was in A.D. 70. At that time they were scattered abroad and there has been no nation of Judah since that day.

The state of Israel was formed in 1948, on the same day that Great Britain gave up the mandate. It is composed of some true blood-stock Jews who are in positions of authority but most of the Israeli population is composed of Gentile Jews of many colours, black, brown and yellow, and also the white Jews from eastern Europe. All these are called Jews because their ancestors accepted the religion of Judah (Judaism).

To see the state of Israel in prophecy we have to turn to Isaiah chapter forty-eight which is addressed to 'the house of Jacob' and so is a message to all Israel, both the house of Israel and the house of Judah. The chapter is divided into three parts. The first part is addressed to the Israeli state as we know it:

> 'Hear ye this, O house of Jacob, which are called by the name of Israel, and are come forth out of the waters of Judah, which swear by the name of the LORD, and make mention of the God of Israel, but not in truth, nor in righteousness. For they call themselves of the holy city, and stay themselves upon the God of Israel; The LORD of hosts is his name.'
>
> Isaiah, ch. 48, vs 1–2

The next verses, three to eleven, are addressed to the house of Judah and tells of their refusal to believe the Lord Jesus Christ when He came. For this refusal they should have been punished by God, but the Lord says:

THE PLAGUES (PART 2)

'Yea, thou heardest not; yea, thou knewest not; yea, from that time that thine ear was not opened: for I knew that thou wouldest deal very treacherously, and wast called a transgressor from the womb. For my name's sake will I defer mine anger, and for my praise will I refrain for thee, that I cut thee not off. Behold, I have refined thee, but not with silver; I have chosen thee in the furnace of affliction. For mine own sake, even for mine own sake, will I do it: for how should my name be polluted? and I will not give my glory unto another.'

Isaiah, ch. 48, vs 8–11

Verses twelve to the end are addressed to the house of Israel and begin 'Hearken unto me, O Jacob and Israel, my called.'

The question now is who, or what, is the nation of Judah, and who will be leading them when all the nations of Europe, the East, and Africa, will be fighting them while they stand firm and will not surrender, even when half the city of Jerusalem is lost to the nations of the world? When we have solved this problem we will be able to see the situation quite clearly.

Before answering these questions, we must clear the ground of all preconceived ideas and the teaching that the Roman Church is the 'man of sin' of second Thessalonians chapter two verse three, or 'the antichrist'.

The Roman Church is the last power of the fourth kingdom of Daniel's image (see Daniel chapter two, and chapter three of this book). Thus, she is named in Revelation chapter seventeen, verse five, as 'BABYLON THE GREAT'. She will be destroyed by the 'ten horns' before the return of the Lord.

'And the ten horns which thou sawest upon the beast, these shall hate the whore, and shall make her desolate and naked, and shall eat her flesh, and burn her with fire.'

Revelation, ch. 17, v. 16

If (as we believe) the whore is the Roman Church then she will be destroyed and for a short time the ten horns will carry on as separate nations before they give their power to the beast (Russia). Thereafter the whole of mainland Europe will go communist and godless and will seek to destroy every church and chapel of every denomination. In fact, they will try to destroy every believer in the Lord Jesus Christ, as the Church universal goes into the last persecution described in Revelation chapter six verses ten and eleven.

As Christianity goes underground the prophecy of Isaiah chapter sixty will be fulfilled:

> 'For, behold, the darkness shall cover the earth, and gross darkness the people . . .'
>
> Isaiah, ch. 60, v. 2

As we have already seen, just before the Coming of the Lord, the united armies of Europe with all their modern weapons will be invading Palestine. All the eastern nations will be doing likewise – a vast array of armies, indeed, multitudes of men and equipment, to use the Bible statement.

> 'For they are the spirits of devils, working miracles, which go forth unto the kings of the earth and of the whole world, to gather them to the battle of that great day of God Almighty.'
>
> Revelation, ch. 16, v. 14

When such a force of arms is set to attack this is enough to scare any nation, however strong it may be. Yet, we see the people of Palestine standing alone, a small nation with few weapons, standing firm and showing no signs of fear. So the question is, 'What makes this nation even attempt to resist?' First, it must have a very strong person who can lead and give the people every confidence that they will win. He must be devil-possessed and a self-deceived fanatic of the worst kind; a man with hypnotic power over the masses. He will be deeply 'religious' in his own cult and a powerful force in the political realm, who will deceive the Jews of the Israeli state.

He is the false prophet (of Revelation chapter sixteen) who helps to bring all the nations down to Palestine. He is the lamb-like creature of Revelation chapter thirteen, verse eleven that suddenly comes into the prophetic picture.

> 'And I beheld another beast coming up out of the earth; and he had two horns like a lamb, and he spake as a dragon.'

THE PLAGUES (PART 2)

Thus, there comes a lamb out of the earth to oppose the Lamb of God at His Coming.

Rome cannot be antichrist, for the antichrist is only mentioned by St. John in his two Epistles. In I John we read:

> 'Little children, it is the last time: and as ye have heard that antichrist shall come, even now are there many antichrists; whereby we know that it is the last time . . . I have not written unto you because ye know not the truth, but because ye know it, and that no lie is of the truth. Who is a liar but he that denieth that Jesus is the Christ? He is antichrist, that denieth the Father and the Son . . . but he that acknowledgeth the Son hath the Father also.'
>
> I John, ch. 2, vs 18 and 21–23

This is a plain statement that the antichrist (which according to Young's Concordance means 'the opposer') is one who denies that Jesus is the Christ. By no evidence can it be proved that the Roman Church has ever denied that Jesus is the Christ. Note that St. John calls such a one a 'liar' – a point to which we shall turn again in another prophecy.

In his second Epistle (verse 7) St. John refers to the antichrist again:

> 'For many deceivers are entered into the world, who confess not that Jesus Christ is come in the flesh. This is a deceiver and an antichrist.'

This again rules out Rome, but notice that the word 'deceiver' ties up with 'liar'.

The only antichrist people throughout the Christian age have been the Jews. However, it is important to understand that the ultimate antichrist is future. The proof is in I John chapter two verse eighteen:

> 'Little children, it is the last time: and as ye have heard that antichrist shall come, even now are there many antichrists; whereby we know that it is the last time.'

Ever since John worded this warning there have been antichrists in every generation of this last time, that is the two thousand years which succeeded the former times, and which will end with the Coming of the Lord. However, the outstanding antichrist who will oppose the Lord at His Second Coming has not yet appeared on the scene.

Nevertheless, once we have seen that Satan has been up to his old trick of deceiving the people in the Church by making them look in the wrong direction, we can know what to look for. We must turn from Church history and study the prophecy relating to the Second Coming if we believe the Second Coming to be the bodily return of the Lord Jesus Christ, for the whole world including the whole Church must change at His Coming. In the same way that the old order of things changed in Jewry at the time of His First Coming. So we must see great changes at His Second Coming. Even the Communion Service must come to an end as the centre of the worship of the true Church, for, the Bible plainly states, 'this do ye, as oft as ye drink it . . . till he come' (I Corinthians, ch. 11, vs 25–26). What the new form of worship will be we will not know till He comes. For one thing, the age-long worship in sections, each section denying the others and accusing them of errors, will pass as all true saints join in true worship. At present, while the Head of the Church is unseen, men follow various seen heads, but when the Head of the Church is seen in our midst, we will need no other leader.

Chapter 8

THE FALSE PROPHET AND JUDGMENT ON LEVI AND JUDAH

WE SAW in the last chapter that the final antichrist must be a leader who will appear at the last stage of the present age. We now turn to the second book of Thessalonians and see not 'the man of sin', but 'that man of sin', who is 'the son of perdition' (destruction – Young's Concordance). First of all we must find the time factor of the prophecy:

> 'And to you who are troubled rest with us, when the Lord Jesus shall be revealed from heaven with his mighty angels, In flaming fire taking vengeance on them that know not God, and that obey not the gospel of our Lord Jesus Christ: Who shall be punished with everlasting destruction from the presence of the Lord, and from the glory of his power; When he shall come to be glorified in his saints, and to be admired in all them that believe . . . in that day. Wherefore also we pray always for you, that our God would count you worthy of this calling, and fulfil all the good pleasure of his goodness, and the work of faith with power: That the name of our Lord Jesus Christ may be glorified in you, and ye in him, according to the grace of our God and the Lord Jesus Christ.'
> II Thessalonians, ch. 1, vs 7–12

We pause here for a moment to see where we stand personally, and pray for our Fellowship and every member, that the Lord Jesus Christ will be glorified in us and that we may all be counted worthy in that day which is now drawing so near. We now continue to read:

> 'Now we beseech you, brethren, by the coming of our Lord Jesus Christ, and by our gathering together unto him (in what is called, "the rapture of the Church"), That ye be not soon shaken in mind, or be troubled, neither by spirit, nor by word, nor by letter as from us, as that the day of Christ is at hand.'
> II Thessalonians, ch. 2, vs 1–2

Many have foolishly predicted the exact time of the Lord's Second Coming, and have been proved wrong. Many have taught and still teach that the Lord may come at any time, saying, "It may be today" (they have said it so often that the hearts of the hearers have waxed cold). They are also wrong because there is a considerable volume of prophecy which must be fulfilled first, and although it could be fulfilled quite quickly it will certainly require several years yet. In fact we do not know when the Lord will return, whether it will be next year, in ten years time, or longer than that, but, whenever He comes we must be ready to meet Him. The Bible tells us clearly that we know not the day or the hour of His Coming, but it also tells us that we can know the times and the seasons. This we can do by the careful study of Bible prophecy, and by rightly dividing the word of truth. So Paul, after warning us against listening to predictions or making predictions concerning the exact time of return of the Lord, goes on to give us two certain signs of that Coming. Here is the first sign:

> 'Let no man deceive you by any means: for that day shall not come, except there come a falling away first . . .'
> II Thessalonians, ch. 2, v. 3

If this means a falling away from the Church (and it seems to us that this is the real meaning), then surely we are seeing it happening now. God says, 'thou hast been weary of me, O Israel. . . . thou hast wearied me with thine iniquities' (Isaiah, ch. 43, vs 22 and 24), and again, 'O my people, what have I done unto thee? and wherein have I wearied thee?' (Micah, ch. 6, v. 3).

There are various reasons for this state of affairs and the following are some. The pleasures of this world are now more easy to come by, with cars, television and other entertainments on the Sabbath. The uncertainty of the message in many churches is another factor as the clergy tear the Bible to pieces and teach sinful ways instead of proclaiming the firm message which the people once understood – 'Thus saith the Lord!' Also there is the ungodly teaching in the schools and the lack of

THE FALSE PROPHET

believing teachers to teach the Bible. Added to this is the popular but erroneous humanist teaching that man is a mighty creature capable of mastering his own destiny. All around us we see the approaching growth of godless communism. Finally, there is the changing of the ways and forms of worship that our forefathers loved, and neglecting to teach the one great truth, 'Ye must be born again', and 'Believe on the Lord Jesus Christ, and thou shalt be saved.'

The second sign is as follows:

> '. . . and that (notice it does not say "the") man of sin be revealed, the son of perdition; Who opposeth and exalteth himself above all that is called God, or that is worshipped . . .'
>
> II Thessalonians, ch. 2, vs 3–4

This description of the son of perdition is somewhat similar to that of the 'king of the north' (see Daniel, ch. 11, v. 36), and their rival claims result in their mounting opposition to each other.

The son of perdition sets himself up as God or, in other words he claims to be the Messiah. The Jews accused the Lord Jesus of claiming to be God when He proclaimed Himself to be the Christ:

> 'I and my Father are one. Then the Jews took up stones again to stone him. Jesus answered them, Many good works have I shewed you from my Father; for which of those works do you stone me? The Jews answered him, saying, For a good work we stone thee not; but for blasphemy; and because that thou, being a man, makest thyself God.'
>
> John, ch. 10, vs 30–33

Thus in the end, there will be two men facing each other; both proud, both working miracles, both vain and egoistical in the extreme. One (the king of the north) is the beast personified, and the other (the son of perdition) is the false prophet. One (the king of the north) depending upon his vast armies, the other (the son of perdition) not on this defence but believing he has supernatural powers by which he must triumph. The son of perdition (who is also 'the false prophet') will rule over Judah in Jerusalem, and will be determined to make the Holy City stand firm. Thus he is described:

> 'Who opposeth and exalteth himself above all that is called God, or that is worshipped; so that he as God sitteth in the temple of God, shewing himself that he is God. Remember ye not, that, when I was yet with you, I told you these things? And now ye know what withholdeth that he might be revealed in his time. For the mystery of iniquity doth already work: only he who now letteth (to hold down, or hold fast) will let, until he be taken out of the way. (We believe that "he" refers to the Holy Ghost). And then shall that Wicked be revealed, whom the Lord shall consume with the spirit of his mouth, and shall destroy with the brightness of his coming:'
> II Thessalonians, ch. 2, vs 4–8

This man will be in existence therefore at the time of the Coming of the Lord and will come face to face with Him. Now let us look again at this evil man:

> 'Even him, whose coming is after the working of Satan with all power and signs and lying wonders, And with all deceivableness of unrighteousness in them that perish; because they received not the love of the truth, that they might be saved.'
> II Thessalonians, ch. 2, vs 9–10

Now we must ask, what is 'the truth' which they would not believe? Is it not that Jesus is God, and that He came in the flesh? Therefore St. John says they are antichrist. Now for judgment. If they refused for two thousand years to believe the truth, the judgment must be a righteous one:

> 'And for this cause (because they would not believe the truth) God shall send them strong delusion, that they should believe a lie: That they all might be damned who believed not the truth, but had pleasure in unrighteousness.'
> II Thessalonians, ch. 2, vs 11–12

This makes it clear that the 'man of sin' will be the leader of Jewry, ruling in Jerusalem, when the Lord returns. He will find it fairly easy to gain power, for over four thousand years ago Israel were told that one day a new Prophet would appear with God-given authority to make changes in the Law of Moses:

THE FALSE PROPHET

> 'The LORD thy God will raise up unto thee a Prophet from the midst of thee, of thy brethren, like unto me; unto him ye shall hearken.'
>
> Deuteronomy, ch. 18, v. 15

Then in verse eighteen the promised Prophet is again the subject, but with a difference:

> 'I will raise them up a Prophet from among their brethren, like unto thee, and will put my words in his mouth; and he shall speak unto them all that I shall command him. And it shall come to pass, that whosoever will not hearken unto my words which he shall speak in my name, I will require it of him.'
>
> (vs 18–19)

After quoting the verse we have just quoted, St. Peter tells us (Acts, ch. 7, v. 37) that, the Lord Jesus Christ was that Prophet and also the long expected Messiah. For nearly two thousand years Christians have accepted the words of Peter, inspired by the Holy Spirit. However, the Jews rejected Him, and so, for the two thousand years of the Christian Age, they have believed that 'the Prophet' would come in the future, and, that the Messiah would also come. Now that the Israeli state has been set up, they believe that the time is at hand for His Coming. It is also a time of trouble and danger, and so they will be eager to accept the false messiah and the false prophet.

This man must be most convincing if he is going to lure Jewry into his power. He must be able to prove his descent from the house of Judah, and from the house of David. There are many Jews in the world today who can prove that they are true Judah, and a few who can prove that they are from the line of David.

When Jewry was about to go into captivity, the Lord finally divided the nation of Israel from the nation of Judah and reaffirmed His covenants with David and the Levites that David's children would reign over the house of Israel, and that the Levites would always be the ministers of the Lord. These covenants were made very binding by the Lord.

> 'For thus saith the LORD; David shall never want a man to sit upon the throne of the house of Israel, Neither shall the priests the Levites want a man before me . . . to do sacrifice continually . . . Thus saith the LORD; If ye can break my covenant of the day, and my covenant of the night, and that there should not be day and night in their season; Then may also my covenant be broken with David my servant, that he should not have a son to reign upon his throne; and with the Levites the priests, my ministers. As the host of heaven cannot be numbered, neither the sand of the sea measured: so will I multiply the seed of David my servant, and the Levites that minister unto me.'
>
> Jeremiah, ch. 33, vs 17–18 and 20–22

Therefore when the Throne of David was removed from Palestine to these Islands the priestly tribe of Levi took over the rulership of Jewry. When the Jews returned to Judea from Babylon, the Levites assumed control of the country, and when the Lord came the Levites were still responsible over Jewry for all internal affairs. Ever since, it has been the Rabbis (the Levites) who have held Jewry together and kept them in the faith of Judaism in many times of distress and persecution. In fact, it is possible that, but for the Rabbis, the Jewish people would have mixed with the other nations and become extinct as a separate race. It was the priesthood who were so bitterly against the Lord and brought about His death, and they have maintained this hatred against the Lord now for nearly two thousand years. (We have met many Jews who have listened with interest while we have told them of the ten lost tribes being found in the Islands, but once we named the Lord Jesus Christ we lost all contact with them.)

With this covenant of the Lord, and all this background in mind, it is easy to see that the house of Judah, and the tribe of Levi, must have an important part to play in the day of the Lord. Therefore, it is not surprising to find that Zechariah writes of the nation that will be in Palestine at the time of the Coming of the Lord:

> 'Behold, I will make Jerusalem a cup of trembling unto all the people round about, when they shall be in the siege both against Judah and

THE FALSE PROPHET

against Jerusalem . . . And the governors of Judah shall say in their heart, The inhabitants of Jerusalem shall be my strength in the LORD of hosts their God.'
Zechariah, ch. 12, vs 2 and 5

Notice that the inhabitants of Jerusalem will still be a mixed Gentile-Jewry. However, once the false prophet declares himself to be the long promised Messiah who will reign in Jerusalem over all the nations of the earth, Jews from all over the world will flock to Palestine, and they will be of the true house of Judah. The Levites will form the administration under the false prophet. Notice also that Judah will be putting their faith in the leader, but he will be relying on the faith of the people of Jerusalem in the Lord their God to keep up their morale in the days of danger!

That the Levites will be there is plain from the book of Malachi:

'Behold, I will send my messenger, and he shall prepare the way before me: and the Lord, whom ye seek, shall suddenly come to his temple, even the messenger of the covenant, whom ye delight in: behold, he shall come, saith the LORD of hosts.'
Malachi, ch. 3, v. 1

We are told by many Bible students that this is a repeat of Isaiah chapter forty and refers to John the Baptist, but, the verses that follow rule this out. The 'messenger' of chapter three must be 'the prophet' of the next chapter which reads:

'Behold, I will send you Elijah the prophet before the coming of the great and dreadful day of the LORD.'
Malachi, ch. 4, v. 5

Thus, two messengers will come. The first messenger will prepare the way of the second, 'the messenger of the covenant', who is the Lord Jesus Christ. The next verse tells us this.

'But who may abide the day of his coming? and who shall stand when he appeareth?'
Malachi, ch. 3, v. 2

When the Lord came the first time He did not suddenly appear in His Temple. He entered as a babe, then as a man He entered it many times during His ministry. He did not come to judge but to save. Now in Malachi chapter three He is coming to judge, and 'who may abide the day of his coming?'

> '... for he is like a refiner's fire, and like fullers' soap: And he shall sit as a refiner and purifier of silver: and he shall purify the sons of Levi, and purge them as gold and silver, that they may offer unto the LORD an offering in righteousness. Then shall the offering of Judah and Jerusalem be pleasant unto the LORD, as in the days of old, and as in former years.'
>
> Malachi, ch. 3, vs 2–4

The fact that the covenant which the Lord made with the house of Levi is still operational now after 2,400 years is proved by the Lord's condemnation of the priests in the previous chapter:

> 'And now, O ye priests, this commandment is for you. If ye will not hear, and if ye will not lay it to heart, to give glory unto my name, saith the LORD of hosts, I will even send a curse upon you, and I will curse your blessings: yea, I have cursed them already, because ye do not lay it to heart . . . And ye shall know that I have sent this commandment unto you, that my covenant might be with Levi, saith the LORD of hosts. My covenant was with him of life and peace;'
>
> Malachi, ch. 2, vs 1–2 and 4–5

At first the Levites were true to the Lord, but later they departed from being the keepers of the Law as the messengers of the Lord. Consequently the Lord judges them:

> 'But ye are departed out of the way; ye have caused many to stumble at the law; ye have corrupted the covenant of Levi, saith the LORD of hosts . . . Have we not all one father? hath not one God created us? why do we deal treacherously every man against his brother, by profaning the covenant of our fathers?'
>
> Malachi, ch. 2, vs 8 and 10

The priestly tribe of Levi must take the blame for the way they have led Jewry since 400 B.C.. They, with Judah, were against the Lord when He came. When Pilate would have

THE FALSE PROPHET

released the Lord Jesus it was mainly the priests who moved among the people and urged them to choose Barabbas (see Mark, ch. 15, v. 11). First Pilate called the chief priests and the rulers and then the people. Then he declared that he had found no fault in Jesus.

> 'And they were instant with loud voices, requiring that he might be crucified. And the voices of them and of the chief priests prevailed.'
> Luke, ch. 23, v. 23

and,

> 'When the chief priests therefore and officers saw him, they cried out, saying, Crucify him, crucify him.'
> John, ch. 19, v. 6

It is plain to see that the Levitical priesthood has been against the Lord for 2,000 years, and it would hardly be justice to gather together a host of Gentile Jews to Jerusalem and cause them to be killed in the last great battle. No! when the Lord comes it will be to judge true Levi and true Judah.

Chapter 9

THE DIVISION OF THE NATIONS

BEFORE we consider the final stages of the conflict we must see the divisions of the nations, made in readiness for the final judgments of the Lord. The nations of the world will include three main communistic blocks: first, the European nations with South America, under Russia; second, the eastern nations under China and Japan; and third, the African nations from Egypt to the borders of Rhodesia. Arabia will be on its own but will fear invasion by Russia. Canada, the U.S.A., Southern Africa, New Zealand, Australia and Great Britain and Ireland, the main nations of the English-speaking world, would all be vulnerable as separate nations; all isolated and open to attack. Therefore, something must be done by God if the Christian world is to stand any chance against the mighty armed forces of the Satanic nations in their attempt to make evil, and godlessness, worldwide. It does not need a Bible student to see this situation developing even now.

We can go to the Bible and see what the Lord will do. The first step to safety in union for Israel must be our reunion with the Lord. The first thing is that the Lord must, and will, bring all Israel into one union. In Micah chapter six we see the Lord pointing out our danger:

> 'Hear ye now what the LORD saith; Arise, contend thou before the mountains (nations), and let the hills (small nations) hear thy voice. Hear ye, O mountains, the LORD's controversy, and ye strong foundations of the earth: for the LORD hath a controversy with his people, and he will plead with Israel.'
>
> Micah, ch. 6, vs 1–2

This is the Lord pleading with Israel to face up to the truth from His standpoint. This point is brought out in the next verse:

THE DIVISION OF THE NATIONS

'O my people, what have I done unto thee? and wherein have I wearied thee? testify against me.'

That this accusation is true cannot be denied. We have as a nation become tired of our God because we have been turned away from God's word. We are taught by churchmen and teachers that the Old Testament is not true. Bible truth is in general being distorted, and the moral code of the Lord is being thrown overboard. So, as we have tired of our God, the Lord asks us to reconsider what He did for us in our dire need in the old days:

> 'For I brought thee up out of the land of Egypt, and redeemed thee out of the house of servants; and I sent before thee Moses, Aaron, and Miriam. O my people, remember now what Balak king of Moab consulted, and what Balaam the son of Beor answered him from Shittim (a place in Moab) unto Gilgal (near Jericho); that ye may know the righteousness of the LORD.'
>
> Micah, ch. 6, vs 4–5

So, in our present weakness, the Lord turns us back to the 'discredited' Old Testament and to the mighty deliverance of the Lord when only two men and one woman formed the defence of the people. Israel had a few weapons when they came out of Egypt, but there was no defence force in Israel. It was not until thirteen months after they came out of Egypt that Moses formed a standing army, and commanded every fit man aged twenty years old and upwards to prepare for war, and to train in their spare time for the nation's defence (just like the Israelis are doing today!). That first standing army of Israel numbered 'six hundred thousand and three thousand and five hundred and fifty' (see Numbers, ch. 2 v. 32). Assuming that the army was twenty-five per cent of all the people, including all the females, old people, and those under twenty (this is probably an over-estimate), then, Moses had to bring about two and a half million people out of Egypt. Surely if we believe this to be true then God has convinced us that we, with Him, can stand up against the whole world. Apparently, we will accept the correction of the Lord, and so, we reply by asking Him what we can do:

> 'Wherewith shall I come before the LORD, and bow myself before the high God? shall I come before him with burnt offerings, with calves of a year old? Will the LORD be pleased with thousands of rams, or with ten thousands of rivers of oil? shall I give my firstborn for my transgression, the fruit of my body for the sin of my soul?'
>
> Micah, ch. 6, vs 6–7

Remember, this was written about 2,700 years ago, when there was no vast quantity of oil in the world known to man. It is only in the last few years that we knew that we would have rivers (pipelines) of oil and now already we are thinking of sharing it with the other nations! We have given our firstborn to preserve world peace and to obtain freedom in two world wars, and the U.S.A. has given them recently in Vietnam. We have fed the hungry in the world and believed (correctly) that we were doing right by so doing. Foolishly we did it to establish our own righteousness rather than in the name of our God and in His Great Name. It will avail us nothing when the crisis comes, and the Lord does not ask us to go on doing it. The next verse gives us the answer from the Lord:

> 'He hath shewed thee, O man, what is good; and what doth the LORD require of thee, but to do justly, and to love mercy, and to walk humbly with thy God?'
>
> Micah, ch. 6, v. 8

God asks for only three things, none of which require sacrifice of any kind. He asks us 'to do justly', not only in the law courts but in every walk of life: to do unto others what we hope they will do unto us, so that all get just dealings, from the least to the greatest. Today, going to court to get justice is so costly that it is often better to put up with injustice even if the case is just. If we followed God's first instruction there would be no disputes about wages, no strikes, and neither would there be a few getting rich to the detriment of the many.

THE DIVISION OF THE NATIONS

Secondly, God asks us 'to love mercy' (to have forbearance towards anyone who is under our jurisdiction, and to have a forgiving disposition). So we have to use mercy in all our actions, forgiving the errors in others, and forgiving the wrongs they do to us. Thirdly, God tells us 'to walk humbly with thy God.' God wants total obedience to His will, so that we will not fall for the worst of all sins, spiritual pride and spiritual conceit. The latter summarize the attitude of the Pharisees, and of many Christians today – 'Thank God I am not as other men.' God says (Philippians, ch. 2, v. 3), 'let each esteem other better than themselves!' These are the qualities which the Lord wants of us.

Walking with God and keeping in step with Him, as each move takes place in the world, is going to be vital in the coming days as evil reaches its climax on earth. We are in the same position as at the time when the Spirit of the Lord put the following words into the mind of the prophet:

> 'Oh that my people had hearkened unto me, and Israel had walked in my ways! I should soon have subdued their enemies, and turned my hand against their adversaries . . . He should have fed them also with the finest of the wheat: and with honey out of the rock should I have satisfied thee.'
>
> Psalm 81, vs 13–14 and 16

In the coming time of world shortage and economic want He will feed us and keep us safe from our enemies, who, mad with hate and lust, will seek our complete destruction. However, this means that we will have to conform to God's plan for our security. This activity is described in Ezekiel chapter thirty-seven, verse sixteen to the end of the chapter. As it is so long, it cannot be quoted in full here, but please read it all. It makes a grand final reading at the end of the day and ensures peaceful sleep:

> 'Say unto them, Thus saith the Lord GOD; Behold, I will take the stick of Joseph, which is in the hand of Ephraim, and the tribes of Israel his fellows, and will put them with him, even with the stick of Judah, and make them one stick, and they shall be one in mine hand. And the sticks whereon thou writest shall be in thine hand before their eyes.

And say unto them, Thus saith the Lord GOD; Behold, I will take the children of Israel from among the heathen, whither they be gone (in the days of empire building), and will gather them on every side, and bring them into their own land: And I will make them one nation in the land upon the mountains of Israel; and one king shall be king to them all . . .'

Ezekiel, ch. 37, vs 19–22

All the separate parts of the Israel Commonwealth will give up their separate parliaments and send their representatives to Britain to administer the whole Israel Commonwealth and to bring these things into being and standardise everything in Israel to God's Laws. This Council will be under the Throne of David which then will be subject to our God. Parliaments and presidents will not be acknowledged by Him. The only authority in Israel which is in accordance with God's revealed will is the House of David, and so, it will come into its own and provide the rulers in the day of the coming of the Lord.

As rulers over Israel, the Throne of David was given no authority to make laws but they had to study the Laws of the Lord and to interpret them aright according to the righteousness of the Lord, and to administer them in justice, and mercy, for the welfare and good of the whole nation. I believe that we are right in saying that this privy Council will not be elected by the Israel nations, but will be appointed by the ruler and will consist of Church and State representatives, for, we read in Micah:

'Therefore will he give them up, until the time that she which travaileth hath brought forth: then the remnant of his brethren shall return unto the children of Israel. And he shall stand and feed in the strength of the LORD, in the majesty of the name of the LORD his God; and they shall abide: for now shall he be great unto the ends of the earth. And this man shall be the peace, when the Assyrian (Micah was writing about 700 B.C. when the Assyrian Empire was the second of the six Babylonian Empires) shall come into our land: and when he shall tread in our palaces, then shall we raise against him seven shepherds, and eight principal men.'

Micah, ch. 5, vs 3–5

THE DIVISION OF THE NATIONS

(This chapter in Micah is about the Lord Jesus Christ and deals with both His First and Second Comings.)

The gathering of all Israel into their own lands will include those of Israel who are on the other side of the English Channel. It will come to pass at the time of great distress, as is recorded in Isaiah:

> 'But now thus saith the LORD that created thee, O Jacob, and he that formed thee, O Israel, Fear not: for I have redeemed thee, I have called thee by thy name; thou art mine. When thou passest through the waters, I will be with thee; and through the rivers, they shall not overflow thee: when thou walkest through the fire, thou shalt not be burned; neither shall the flame kindle upon thee. For I am the LORD thy God, the Holy One of Israel, thy Saviour: . . . Fear not: for I am with thee: I will bring thy seed from the east, and gather thee from the west; I will say to the north, Give up; and to the south, Keep not back: bring my sons from far, and my daughters from the ends of the earth; Even every one that is called by my name: for I have created him for my glory, I have formed him; yea, I have made him.'
> Isaiah, ch. 43, vs 1–3 and 5–7

We know that there are many of Israel stock living in all lands who have settled down, bought land and built houses. They will not want to be uprooted, even when they are in danger. They will be willing to take the risk of staying because they believe they have everything to lose by coming out, but, they will have to obey the Lord!

> 'Behold, I will send for many fishers, saith the LORD, and they shall fish them; and after will I send for many hunters, and they shall hunt them from every mountain, and from every hill, and out of the holes of the rocks.'
> Jeremiah, ch. 16, v. 16

So first they will be enticed but later they will be compelled to come out. It is easy to see that these will then all settle down in Israel lands, for we will all be under the New Covenant that our Lord won for us by His death upon the Cross for our salvation. This is the national salvation about which St. Paul writes in Romans:

> 'And so all Israel shall be saved. as it is written, There shall come out of Sion the Deliverer, and shall turn away ungodliness from Jacob.'
>
> Romans, ch. 11, v. 26

St. Paul gives the time of this deliverance as, 'until the fulness of the Gentiles be come in' (v. 25), that is, at the time of the nearness of the Coming of the Lord. This act of God is His saving Israel from the ungodliness of the world, and is not to be confused with the personal salvation which the Lord offers to all who believe in His Name.

In both Jeremiah chapter thirty-two and in Hebrews there is given the text of the New Covenant. We are quoting from Hebrews:

> 'For this is the covenant that I will make with the house of Israel after those days, saith the Lord; I will put my laws into their mind, and write them in their hearts: and I will be to them a God, and they shall be to me a people: And they shall not teach every man his neighbour, and every man his brother, saying, Know the Lord: for all shall know me, from the least to the greatest. For I will be merciful to their unrighteousness, and their sins and their iniquities will I remember no more.'
>
> Hebrews, ch. 8, vs 10–12

This covenant is not written in legal jargon but is given in plain language which everyone can read and understand. The question is, do we believe it? Remember, the Lord made this covenant about 2,600 years ago, long before the Lord Jesus Christ came to the earth (Jeremiah chapter thirty-two). At that time He knew all the sins that Israel would commit and how they would turn away from Him. Moreover, the covenant was repeated after the Lord had paid the price for our sins (Hebrews chapter eight). The Lord did not leave Himself a single loophole so that He could avoid having to keep the covenant for, it is an everlasting covenant and it is based on the everlasting love of the Lord.

> 'The LORD hath appeared of old unto me, saying, Yea, I have loved thee with an everlasting love: therefore with lovingkindness have I drawn thee . . . Hear the word of the LORD, O ye nations, and declare it in the isles afar off, and say, He that scattered Israel will

gather him, and keep him, as a shepherd doth his flock. For the LORD hath redeemed Jacob, and ransomed him from the hand of him that was stronger than he.'
>
> Jeremiah, ch. 31, vs 3, 10 and 11

However, in Jeremiah chapter thirty (the chapter that deals with Jacob's trouble) we read:

> 'And ye shall be my people, and I will be your God. Behold, the whirlwind of the LORD goeth forth with fury, a continuing whirlwind: it shall fall with pain upon the head of the wicked. The fierce anger of the LORD shall not return, until he have done it, and until he have performed the intents of his heart: in the latter days ye shall consider it.'
>
> Jeremiah, ch. 30, vs 22–24

The terrible day of the Lord is a day not wanted by the Lord, who would have all men to be saved, but, it is a vital work that He must perform to bring the world into a state of peace for the whole future of mankind. The Lord has been very tolerant with the nations, and still is being very patient with them, but the results are terrible and the whole world is going into rank ungodliness. Consequently the lesson they have to learn must be the righteousness of the Lord, and also, that He must have His right place in the affairs of men.

> 'With my soul have I desired thee in the night; yea, with my spirit within me will I seek thee early: for when thy judgments are in the earth, the inhabitants of the world will learn righteousness. Let favour be shewed to the wicked, yet will he not learn righteousness: in the land of uprightness will he deal unjustly, and will not behold the majesty of the LORD, LORD when thy hand is lifted up, they will not see: but they shall see, and be ashamed for their envy at the people; yea, the fire of thine enemies shall devour them. LORD, thou wilt ordain (appoint) peace for us: for thou also hast wrought all our works in us.'
>
> Isaiah, ch. 26, vs 9–12

The first act of the Lord is to bring Israel to Himself, and they will willingly become subject to His Law. They will be witnessing to the glory of the Lord in an anti-God world. Of course, the devil will be seeking to exterminate Israel by making war with her because of this strong witness:

> 'And the dragon was wroth with the woman, and went to make war with the remnant of her seed, which keep the commandments of God, and have the testimony of Jesus Christ.'
>
> Revelation, ch. 12, v. 17

All the Lord wants us to do is to have absolute faith and to leave everything to Him during the events of this dreadful time. Even the great desolations will be shown to Israel after they have taken place, to show us, not only what the Lord has done, but why He has done it:

> 'Come, behold the works of the LORD, what desolations he hath made in the earth. He maketh wars to cease unto the end of the earth; he breaketh the bow, and cutteth the spear in sunder; he burneth the chariot in the fire. Be still, and know that I am God: I will be exalted among the heathen, I will be exalted in the earth. The LORD of hosts is with us; the God of Jacob is our refuge.'
>
> Psalm 46, vs 8–11

In that day we will all know the Lord. We will not be in a fearful state of panic no matter how strong are the forces of evil against us, for we are told:

> 'For thus saith the Lord GOD, the Holy One of Israel; In returning and rest shall ye be saved; in quietness and in confidence shall be your strength . . .'
>
> Isaiah, ch. 30, v. 15

It is for us to experience and to know these things. We should be humble and grateful to the Lord for His goodness to us. Our confidence and quietness should inspire others who have not been blessed as we have. When they ask us why we have such a placid attitude, we can witness to the salvation of the Lord Jesus Christ and Him crucified, that they too may know both the peace of having sins forgiven and that the Lord is our great defence against all evil. Soon they will be willing to listen, for the great and terrible day of the Lord is very near.

Chapter 10

SIGHTS OF THE FUTURE

WE HAVE now studied all the main events leading up to the Coming of the Lord. Now we have to study the final scenes, and are waiting for future events and for special people who will arise and play an important part in the Gentile world and have control of the nations of the world when the Lord shall descend from heaven with His angels and saints.

First, we have to see the cleansing of the Chambers before we can close our doors. This means that all the heathen (white or coloured) and all those who believe in communism and are not part of Israel stock, will have to leave the Anglo-Saxon-Celtic parts of the world. This will be the work of the Holy Spirit and the angels as we learn from the parables of the fish net and the wheat and the tares. How they will do it we do not know. It may be when the whole outside world goes communist and Russia attempts to make war with us, for we will be stubbornly resisting and the Bible says that Satan will urge Russia to make war with us. That Russia will not invade us is sure, but, the fear of invasion may be enough to clear the lands of the non-Israelite and non-Christian stock. At the same time, all the Israel stock in the Gentile world will leave and enter into the Israel chambers. They will come under the protection of the Almighty as they move out of the world to come into the place of safety (see Revelation, ch. 12, v. 14, Isaiah, ch. 52, v. 11 and Isaiah, ch. 43, v. 6).

> 'For, lo, I will command, and I will sift the house of Israel among all nations, like as corn is sifted in a sieve, yet shall not the least grain fall upon the earth.'
>
> Amos, ch. 9, v. 9

At the same time, the Lord will cleanse us from all our sins and wickedness, and we will become an holy nation, keeping the Law of the Lord, and stoutly defending the Christian faith; in fact the only people on earth who will be standing for the truth as it is in the Lord Jesus Christ.

There will also be the rise of the four powerful leaders of those who are against the Lord, and these will be alive at the time of His appearing. We know something about them even now. For example, we know the places in which they will appear, but the identity of these men is still hidden in the future. When they are all on the scene we will know that the return of the Lord is near. These four men are:

(a) Gog, the chief prince of Meshech and Tubal (Russia).
(b) 'The ravenous bird' from the East (China and Japan).
(c) 'The false prophet', the leader of Judah in Jerusalem, who will be defying the armies of the world.
(d) 'The king of the south', a prince of Mecca who will unite the true Arab nations south of Palestine, as Russia seeks to invade them after taking Palestine.

We will also see the gathering of the saints of the old and new ages (the true Church) who will be resurrected, and those who are alive changed, and all caught up to meet the Lord in the air and then to come down with Him. However, first of all let us look at Isaiah chapter forty-eight. This chapter is divided into three parts. The first two verses apply to the Israeli state, which is composed of a mixture of true and Gentile Jews. In fact the latter are of all colours, white, black, brown and yellow. These are holding the land of Palestine until the time comes when the fear of invasion will make many of them flee to their own lands. Many will not get away because of the armies surrounding that country.

It is also a fact that all over the world in every land there are small sections of true Judah stock with their synagogues under

SIGHTS OF THE FUTURE

the priesthood of the Levites, thus fulfilling the covenant recorded in Jeremiah that the Lord made with the tribe of Levi, which covers all the ages:

> 'For thus saith the LORD; David shall never want a man to sit upon the throne of the house of Israel; Neither shall the priests the Levites want a man before me to offer burnt offerings . . . Thus saith the LORD; If ye can break my covenant of the day, and my covenant of the night, and that there should not be day and night in their season; Then may also my covenant be broken with David my servant, that he should not have a son to reign upon his throne; and with the Levites the priests, my ministers. As the host of heaven cannot be numbered, neither the sand of the sea measured: so will I multiply the seed of David my servant, and the Levites that minister unto me.'
> Jeremiah, ch. 33, vs 17–18 and 20–22

In the Old Testament days the only place of real contact with God was in the Temple, and wherever Israelites were, they were told to face the Temple when in prayer. Then the Lord would hear their prayers and answer them. It was not until the Lord Jesus Christ died, rose and ascended, that the place of worship was altered to the throne of the Lord in heaven with the Lord Jesus Christ as the only High Priest. Meanwhile the Levites were to be the overseers of Judah. All through the ages of Jewry's persecutions, it has been the Levitical priesthood which has kept them together and distinct. Both the true Jew and the Gentile Jew, who has accepted the religion of Judaism, are separated from the rest of the world. They are a people apart, because of their customs, social ways, food and days of worship. They are Christ rejectors, and the few that become Christians are spurned by their families. They are still looking for the coming of the Messiah who will bring in the age of peace and give them victory over all their enemies, and make them a great nation governing the world from Jerusalem.

Moving on to the second part of Isaiah chapter forty-eight we read:

> 'I have declared the former things from the beginning; and they went forth out of my mouth, and I shewed them; I did them suddenly, and

they came to pass. Because I knew that thou art obstinate, and thy neck is an iron sinew, and thy brow brass; I have even from the beginning declared it to thee; before it came to pass I shewed it thee: lest thou shouldest say, Mine idol hath done them, and my graven image, and my molten image, hath commanded them . . . Yea, thou heardest not; yea, thou knewest not; yea, from that time that thine ear was not opened (when the Lord came): for I knew that thou wouldest deal very treacherously, and wast called a transgressor from the womb.'

Isaiah, ch. 48, vs 3–5 and 8

Now we turn to the New Testament and read why the Lord suddenly turned from plain speech to parables, as recorded in Matthew:

'And the disciples came, and said unto him, Why speakest thou unto them in parables? He answered and said unto them, Because it is given unto you to know the mysteries of the kingdom of heaven, but to them it is not given . . . Therefore speak I to them in parables: because they seeing see not; and hearing they hear not, neither do they understand. And in them is fulfilled the prophecy of Esaias, which saith, By hearing ye shall hear, and shall not understand; and seeing ye shall see, and shall not perceive: For this people's heart is waxed gross, and their ears are dull of hearing, and their eyes they have closed; lest at any time (this covers nearly two thousand years) they should see with their eyes, and hear with their ears, and should understand with their heart, and should be converted, and I should heal them.'

Matthew, ch. 13, vs. 10–11 and 13–15

The onus was, and is, on them to open their eyes, and hear, but the Lord knew they would not do so, and that they would refuse to be converted to the truth, and so, the Lord could not heal them.

Returning again to Isaiah we read:

'For my name's sake will I defer mine anger, and for my praise will I refrain for thee, that I cut thee not off. Behold, I have refined thee, but not with silver; I have chosen thee in the furnace of affliction.'

Isaiah, ch. 48, vs 9–10

The Kingdom cannot go outside the tribes of Israel. We are told that He (Jesus) came unto His own, and His own received Him not. He speaks a parable to the Jews, 'The kingdom of God

SIGHTS OF THE FUTURE

shall be taken from you, and given to a nation bringing forth the fruits thereof' (Matthew, ch. 21, v. 43). Again, St. Paul says, 'What advantage then hath the Jew? . . . Much every way: chiefly, because that unto them were committed the oracles of God' (Romans, ch. 3, vs. 1 and 2). It is a fundamental fact that the Kingdom of God is the Israel people. All other nations are the nations of Satan's realm. We must not let our prejudices lead us into error. It was true Judah, and true Levi, who were in control of Judea in the days of the Lord. To say that it was the Gentile Jews, is to say that the Kingdom of God had already gone into Gentile hands. If this were true it would destroy not only the British Israel case, but also give the lie to the Bible.

It is true that the Idumean Jew was also in the land of Palestine at the time of our Lord's earthly ministry, and that true Judah was mixed up with the Sadducees who denied both the resurrection, and the existence of angels and spirits.

Idumean Jews have had great influence over Jewry even until recent years. It was an Idumean Jew (Lenin) who was sent by the Kaiser to Russia to start the revolution that would take Russia out of the war in 1917. Since then they have become very powerful (see Obadiah, first six verses). It was not a coincidence that Satan began his final bid to take over the world in the same year that the times of the Gentiles came to an end (1917).

It would not be the justice of heaven to punish Gentile Jewry alone for unbelief in the Lord Jesus while leaving true Judah and Levi free from the judgment. Both will have their part in the great battle of the Lord. They both have a hatred of the Lord Jesus Christ deep in their hearts.

We must look deeper into prophecy to see who will be in Palestine when the Lord returns. In Malachi chapter three we read (v. 1):

> 'Behold, I will send my messenger, and he shall prepare the way before me . . .'

Many commentators have said that this was John the Baptist, but it is easy to see that it cannot be, and therefore it must refer to someone else. As the Lord had a messenger before His First Coming, there is also a messenger before His Second Coming. Continuing to read, we find it is judgment that is the picture. When He came the first time the Lord said He had not come to judge but to save! So we now read:

> '. . . and the Lord, whom ye seek, shall suddenly come to his temple, even the messenger of the covenant, whom ye delight in: behold, he shall come, saith the LORD of hosts.'
>
> Malachi, ch. 3, v. 1

The messenger is named in the last chapter:

> 'Behold, I will send you Elijah the prophet before the coming of the great and dreadful day of the LORD: And he shall turn the heart of the fathers to the children, and the heart of the children to their fathers, lest I come and smite the earth with a curse.'
>
> Malachi, ch. 4, vs 5–6

We now continue to read in chapter three:

> 'But who may abide the day of his coming? and who shall stand when he appeareth? for he is like a refiner's fire, and like fullers' soap: And he shall sit as a refiner and purifier of silver: and he shall purify the sons of Levi, and purge them as gold and silver, that they may offer unto the LORD an offering in righteousness. Then shall the offering of Judah and Jerusalem be pleasant unto the LORD, as in the days of old, and as in former years. And I will come near to you to judgment . . .'
>
> Malachi, ch. 3, vs 2–5

This clearly shows that the prophecy takes place at the time of the Second Coming of the Lord, and that it applies to Levi, Judah and Jerusalem. Again we read:

> 'Behold, I will make Jerusalem a cup of trembling unto all the people round about, when they shall be in the siege both against Judah and against Jerusalem.'
>
> Zechariah, ch. 12, v. 12

SIGHTS OF THE FUTURE

> 'And Judah also shall fight at Jerusalem; and the wealth of all the heathen round about shall be gathered together, gold, and silver, and apparel, in great abundance.'
>
> Zechariah, ch. 14, v. 14

> 'I will also stretch out mine hand upon Judah, and upon all the inhabitants of Jerusalem . . . Therefore their goods shall become a booty, and their houses a desolation: they shall also build houses, but not inhabit them; and they shall plant vineyards, but not drink the wine thereof. The great day of the LORD is near, it is near, and hasteth greatly, even the voice of the day of the LORD: the mighty man shall cry there bitterly.'
>
> Zephaniah, ch. 1, vs 4, 13 and 14

Now this verse does not apply to the Israelis of today. They have built houses and lived in them, and they have planted vineyards and drunk the wine thereof. This refers to true Judah who at a later time will flock to Jerusalem. The true Jews will return in large numbers in the day when the antichrist will arise and declare himself to be the saviour of his people, though all the world be gathered against Jerusalem. Already large numbers of Jews in the U.S.A. are being trained in the use of weapons of war, during the holiday periods from schools and colleges, supposedly to defend themselves against possible persecution. It is all a quite legal activity, but when the call comes they could flock to Jerusalem to defend the city against an invader. Be that as it may, just before the Lord returns, from all over the world Judah will go to defend Palestine, counting it an honour to serve under (as they believe) the long awaited Messiah.

Now we turn to Matthew where we read:

> 'When ye therefore shall see the abomination of desolation, spoken of by Daniel the prophet, stand in the holy place, /whoso readeth, let him understand:/ Then let them which be in Judaea flee into the mountains:'
>
> Matthew, ch. 24, vs 15–16

Here is one of the last signs of the Lord's return, for it is fulfilled at the time of His Coming in judgment.

We must always bear in mind that the Lord spent three years teaching the people and during that time He must have given many long discourses, but not one of them is given to us in full in the Gospels. Each of the gospel writers was inspired by the Holy Spirit to present a different aspect of our Lord's ministry and each uses part of the discourses or acts of the Lord, as evidence. Matthew sets out to present the Lord in His Kingship, and so he starts with the wise men visiting the baby King. Mark presents the Lord as the servant of the Kingdom doing the special work which He alone had to do. He is not concerned with the birth but after stating, 'The beginning of the gospel of Jesus Christ, the Son of God' goes directly to the baptism of Jesus. Luke on the other hand presented Jesus in His manhood, and so he deals with the birth of our Lord, and the visit of the shepherds to see the Lamb of God; while John had to show the deity of Jesus, and so he starts off with, 'In the beginning was the Word, and the Word was with God, and the Word was God . . . And the Word was made flesh, and dwelt among us' (John, ch. 1, vs 1 and 14).

We have pointed this out now because each Evangelist used only parts of the discourse to prove his case. So Mark uses an extra statement made by the Lord that is omitted by Matthew. It may have been from a different discourse, as the Lord may have given several addresses on the same subject.

> 'But when ye shall see the abomination of desolation, spoken of by Daniel the prophet, standing where it ought not, /let him that readeth understand,/ then let them that be in Judaea flee to the mountains:'
> Mark, ch. 13, v. 14

So in Matthew 'the abomination' is standing in the Holy Place, but in Mark it is standing in the place 'where it ought not'. This one point explains the case, so that the wise can understand.

Daniel gives the abomination in the place where it should not be:

> 'And he shall plant the tabernacles of his palace between the seas in the glorious holy mountain; yet he shall come to his end, and none shall help him.'
>
> Daniel, ch. 11, v. 45

This means that he is at war; for when Israel was at peace they lived in houses, but when at war, the order was, 'to your tents, O Israel' (I Kings, ch. 12, v. 16). His palace would be in Jerusalem but the tents were on the Mount of Olives, the Jewish leader having lost half the city of Jerusalem is making his last stand with the remains of his army on the Temple mount.

The one thing that stands out quite clearly is that the 'man of sin' is in charge at the time of 'the abomination'. Therefore 'the abomination' cannot be the Church of Rome, nor can it be the Mosque of Omar, which is in Jerusalem, as this is not a tent (tabernacle) and cannot be moved. It is yet possible that the Mosque of Omar can be destroyed. It is in a dangerous spot with all the fighting that is going on at intervals between the Jews and their enemies. The abominator must be a man who first proclaims himself to be the Messiah, perhaps in a hurried structure erected on the Temple site. This he will do before the invasion by the armies of the nations.

He must be the man that St. Paul tells us about (in the Second book of Thessalonians) when he warns us not to believe anything we hear about the Lord's return, but to watch events that will be taking place, and the rise of the antichrist, who (according to St. John) denies that Jesus is the Christ and denies that Jesus Christ has come in the flesh. He must be the 'false prophet' of Revelation chapter thirteen who, together with the dragon (Satan) and the beast (Gog), brings the whole world to the battle of the great day of God Almighty.

One of the first signs of these events is given by St. Paul, namely:

> 'Let no man deceive you by any means: for that day shall not come, except there come a falling away first . . .'
>
> II Thessalonians, ch. 2, v. 3

This sign will be plainly seen and it has already started in the Church. However, the churches may yet be filled in the time of the awakening, but when the world goes communist then there will be a great falling away as the people become godless. This can now be seen in the nations behind the iron curtain and in many other heathen nations who are forcing missionary activities to be shut down.

> '... and that man of sin be revealed, the son of perdition; Who opposeth and exalteth himself above all that is called God, or that is worshipped; so that he as God sitteth in the temple of God, shewing himself that he is God.'
>
> II Thessalonians, ch. 2, vs 3–4

The name 'the son of perdition' is only given to one other man in the Bible, and it was used by the Lord.

> 'While I was with them in the world, I kept them in thy name: those that thou gavest me I have kept, and none of them is lost, but the son of perdition; that the scripture might be fulfilled.'
>
> John, ch. 17, v. 12

Second Thessalonians reads:

> 'And then shall that Wicked be revealed, whom the Lord shall consume with the spirit of his mouth, and shall destroy with the brightness of his coming.'
>
> II Thessalonians, ch. 2, v. 8

This man will have to prove that he is of the tribe of Judah, and of the house of David. This point is brought out very strongly, but further consideration of this man must be left until a later chapter (see Chapter 19, pp. 164–166).

Chapter 11

A STUDY OF ISAIAH CHAPTER FORTY-TWO

ONE of the most confusing passages in the Bible for believers, and used by those who say that the Bible is not inspired and contradicts itself, is this, the opening words of Isaiah chapter forty-two:

> 'Behold my servant, whom I uphold; mine elect, in whom my soul delighteth; I have put my spirit upon him: he shall bring forth judgment to the Gentiles. He shall not cry, nor lift up, nor cause his voice to be heard in the street.'
>
> Isaiah, ch. 42, vs 1–2

The critics say that the Lord Jesus, to whom this passage must refer, did lift up His voice in the street. In fact, for three years during the whole of His ministry He openly addressed crowds in the streets and in the open, sometimes speaking to thousands at a time. Therefore, they say the Bible is unreliable and cannot be accepted as being inspired or even the truth.

These critics do not notice the part of the text which is the key-note of the explanation: 'he shall bring forth judgment to the Gentiles.' During His ministry the Lord said to his disciples, 'Go not into the way of the Gentiles,' (Matthew, ch. 10, v. 5), and of Himself He said, 'I am not sent but unto the lost sheep of the house of Israel' (Matthew, ch. 15, v. 24). So the passage from Isaiah was for a later time after His work on earth was finished and He had ascended into heaven. Today the Lord Jesus is seated at the right hand of the Father, but the Christ is still operating on the earth. The unseen presence of the Lord is always with us as He promised 'lo, I am with you alway, even unto the end of the world (age).' (Matthew, ch. 28, v. 20).

For nearly two thousand years He has been engaged in the great work of preparing to win the world to Himself, and during the whole of that time He has not been heard in the street, or lifted up His voice, not even in judgment. The next verse states:

> 'A bruised reed shall he not break, and the smoking flax shall he not quench: he shall bring forth judgment unto truth.'
>
> Isaiah, ch. 42, v. 3

Ever since He went into heaven He has carried out His mission, as He said, He did not come to judge at His First Coming.

> 'And if any man hear my words, and believe not, I judge him not: for I came not to judge the world, but to save the world. He that rejecteth me, and receiveth not my words, hath one that judgeth him: the word that I have spoken, the same shall judge him in the last day.'
>
> John, ch. 12, vs 47–48

For two thousand years the Lord has been dealing very gently with those who will not accept Him. If they show any interest in the truth, but are as a bruised reed, the Lord will handle that person so carefully that the reed will not break but be made strong. Any person who shows some belief in the Lord will be like the smoking flax. The Lord will not let it die out but will gently fan it until he is a shining light for the Lord. This has been going on in all the generations of the Christian age, and yet not once has His voice been heard in the street.

The next verse is one of assurance. In spite of the Gentiles who show no real interest in the Lord, He will persevere until He succeeds:

> 'He shall not fail nor be discouraged, till he have set judgment in the earth: and the isles shall wait for his law.'
>
> Isaiah, ch. 42, v. 4

Notice the two different parts of this verse; the first applies to the Gentiles, and the second refers to Israel in the Islands. One shows the determination of the Lord, and the other shows the plan of God. The Law will not be fully kept until that time.

The Islands have the gospel of the Lord Jesus Christ and so are under grace, but the full Law will be delayed according to the prophecy of Malachi.

> 'Remember ye the law of Moses my servant, which I commanded unto him in Horeb for all Israel, with the statutes and judgments. Behold, I will send you Elijah the prophet before the coming of the great and dreadful day of the LORD: And he shall turn the heart of the fathers to the children, and the heart of the children to their fathers, lest I come and smite the earth with a curse.'
> Malachi, ch. 4, vs 4–6

St. Paul brought this point into the open when he wrote:

> 'For I would not, brethren, that ye should be ignorant of this mystery, lest ye should be wise in your own conceits; that blindness in part is happened to Israel, until the fulness of the Gentiles be come in. And so all Israel shall be saved: as it is written, There shall come out of Sion the Deliverer, and shall turn away ungodliness from Jacob: For this is my covenant unto them, when I shall take away their sins.'
> Romans, ch. 11, vs 25–27

Returning to Isaiah chapter forty-two, the prophet now gives a fourfold declaration of God's action and intent showing that the infallible will of God, and the prophecy, must be fulfilled.

> 'Thus saith God the LORD, (a) he that created the heavens, and stretched them out; (b) he that spread forth the earth, and that which cometh out of it; (c) he that giveth breath unto the people upon it, (d) and spirit to them that walk therein.'
> Isaiah, ch. 42, v. 5

The next three verses apply to the one who has been silent for so long.

> 'I the LORD have called thee in righteousness, and will hold thine hand, and will keep thee, and give thee for a covenant of the people, for a light of the Gentiles.'
> Isaiah, ch. 42, v. 6

Again notice the dual work of the servant (the silent one of verse one), first to be the covenant to the people (Israel), and then to be the light of the Gentiles.

> 'To open the blind eyes, to bring out the prisoners from the prison, and them that sit in darkness out of the prison house.'
>
> Isaiah, ch. 42, v. 7

Today, there are thousands of believers in prison in heathen lands and in communist countries, and thousands more who live in those lands who are in danger of imprisonment. The situation will become far worse in the whole of the Gentile world the nearer we get to the great dividing of the nations before the judgments of the Lord are in the earth. The Lord declares that He will not give His glory to any other, be they dictators, or images, or both!

> 'I am the LORD: that is my name: and my glory will I not give to another, neither my praise to graven images.'
>
> Isaiah, ch. 42, v. 8

The next verse (nine) brings us up to date as the Lord tells us what He intends to do to establish His Name among the heathen. As usual, He states the new thing which He is going to do before it comes to pass, so that the believers will see the end product and keep their faith in Him when all seems to be going wrong.

In the next verse (ten) Israel is told of the new song she will sing during the Christian age:

> 'Sing unto the LORD a new song, and his praise from the end of the earth, ye that go down to the sea, and all that is therein; the isles, and the inhabitants thereof.'
>
> Isaiah, ch. 42, v. 10

In the Old Testament days Israel sang the song of Moses, but now we sing the new song in the Psalms.

> 'O sing unto the LORD a new song: sing unto the LORD, all the earth. Sing unto the LORD, bless his name; shew forth his salvation from day to day . . . Before the Lord: for he cometh, for he cometh to judge the earth: he shall judge the world with righteousness, and the people with his truth.'
>
> Psalm 96, vs 1–2 and 13

Thus, the song that Israel will be singing, as a witness to the ends of the earth, is the song of the Lamb.

We now pass on to verses twelve to fourteen of Isaiah chapter forty-two:

> 'Let them give glory unto the LORD, and declare his praise in the islands. The LORD shall go forth as a mighty man, he shall stir up jealousy like a man of war: he shall cry, yea, roar: he shall prevail against his enemies. I have long time holden my peace; I have been still, and refrained myself; now will I cry like a travailing woman; I will destroy and devour at once.'

Thus, the time of silence of the first verse has come to an end. The Lord has been long-suffering with the world for nearly two thousand years, and has not shown His mighty power in spite of all the attacks that have been made against Him. Now the time of judgment has come, and He will keep silent no longer. As usual, when we have a passage that deals with these terrible events of the judgments of the Lord, He tells us the reason for them, so that the believers will not be worried and lose faith. The judgments of the Lord are just and righteous:

> '. . . I will destroy and devour at once. I will make waste mountains and hills, and dry up all their herbs; and I will make the rivers islands, and I will dry up the pools.'
> Isaiah, ch. 42, vs. 14–15

There are many passages in the Bible that tell of the great disturbance which will take place at that time, now drawing so close. First we turn to Psalm forty-six to see that the demolition is so that this present evil age will be replaced by something far better. So that Israel will know beforehand what will happen, and will be full of faith at the time, God proclaims this truth:

> 'God is our refuge and strength, a very present help in trouble. Therefore will not we fear . . .'
> Psalm 46, vs 1–2

Now follow the events that could cause the fear: the earth removed; the mountains carried away into the sea; the waters roar and are troubled; the mountains shake; but these are all necessary for the great age that is to follow:

> 'There is a river, the streams whereof shall make glad the city of God, the holy place of the tabernacles of the most High. God is in the midst of her; she shall not be moved . . .'
>
> Psalm 46, vs 4–5

One cannot imagine the Lord coming to take over Jerusalem as it is today. Next, the Psalmist tells us of the wickedness of the Gentiles.

> 'The heathen raged, the kingdoms were moved: he uttered his voice (after the long silence), the earth melted. The LORD of hosts is with us; the God of Jacob is our refuge. Come, behold the works of the LORD, what desolations he hath made in the earth. He maketh wars to cease . . .'
>
> Psalm 46, vs 6–9

All the Lord is asking us to do during this terrible upheaval and battle is, 'Be still and know that I am God:' (v. 10).

Again we turn back to Isaiah chapter forty-two and read:

> 'And I will bring the blind by a way that they knew not; I will lead them in paths that they have not known: I will make darkness light before them, and crooked things straight. These things will I do unto them, and not forsake them. They shall be turned back, they shall be greatly ashamed, that trust in graven images, that say to the molten images, Ye are our gods.'
>
> Isaiah, ch. 42, vs 16–17

The Lord has already led us by a way we have not known. In this He has directed our paths towards these Islands and to the other parts of the world, in fact, to the ends of the earth, to form the other Israel nations. After we left Palestine, we entered the time of darkness, and we were lost among the nations and worshipped their idols. However, the Lord led us out of our darkness, first bringing us to the Islands, and then into the gospel of the Lord Jesus Christ. With this light we were built up into a nation, and a company of nations, and the great people of the U.S.A., who left these Islands that they might have greater freedom to worship the Lord. One German said, "The British people grew up by accident, and not by design, and so they can be broken down." He did not know that Britain's growth had been well planned, not by us, but by the Lord God of Israel! He planned it, not for us to boast, but to glorify Himself. Although we have given the Empire away and turned from the Lord, He will still prevail and He will cause us to glorify Him in the world. We are still blind, both to the fact of our identity, and to the fact that we are God's people, and so we do not know the real reason for our existence. The following verses tell us this:

> 'Hear, ye deaf; and look, ye blind, that ye may see. Who is blind, but my servant? or deaf, as my messenger that I sent? who is blind as he that is perfect (Hebrew, to be completed), and blind as the LORD's servant? Seeing many things, but thou observest not; opening the ears, but he heareth not. The LORD is well pleased for his righteousness' sake; he will magnify the law, and make it honourable.'
> Isaiah, ch. 42, vs 18–21

This is a strange statement. The Lord is well pleased because Israel is deaf and blind, but as usual, with the Bible, it is easy to understand. During the Old Testament days Israel knew who she was and had the prophets to tell her the will of the Lord who, with a mighty hand, brought her out of Egypt to be a people unto Himself: but, they were a rebellious people, and wanted to be like the heathen nations, and so the Lord apparently sent them to drift among the Gentile nations not knowing if they could survive. However, the Lord had not forsaken them. So we read that all the time He was leading them in the right paths, and, although they were separated into small nations, they were all being led to the same place.

> '. . . and she went after her lovers, and forgat me, saith the LORD. Therefore, behold, I will allure her, and bring her into the wilderness, and speak comfortably unto her.'
> Hosea, ch. 2, vs 13–14

The question is, "Where is the wilderness?" It cannot be Palestine. It is certainly a place of safety, and it is a land in which there are no wild beasts.

> 'And I will make with them a covenant of peace, and will cause the evil beasts to cease out of the land: and they shall dwell safely in the wilderness, and sleep in the woods.'
>
> Ezekiel, ch. 34, v. 25

The theme of Hosea chapter two is also taken up by Ezekiel:

> 'And I will bring you out from the people, and will gather you out of the countries wherein ye are scattered, with a mighty hand, and with a stretched out arm, and with fury poured out. And I will bring you into the wilderness of the people, and there will I plead with you face to face.'
>
> Ezekiel, ch. 20, vs 34–35

Although we came into the wilderness (which is also termed our 'chambers') it does not mean that our eyes and ears are open. This comes after some time, and it is yet future. We are still waiting for the day to come. Whilst we are blind, and deaf, God can lead us according to His will, and He can forgive us for going astray and mixing with the other nations, and for putting our trust in them and not in Him. If our eyes were opened and we then went astray, we would have to pay the price for our sins. St. Paul preached the gospel of the Lord Jesus Christ to the Athenians who had images to every known heathen god, and who to be on the safe side, had one for the worship of the unknown god. Towards the end of the address he said:

> 'And the times of this ignorance God winked at; but now commandeth all men every where to repent.'
>
> Acts, ch. 17, v. 30

In exactly the same way the Lord can be tolerant with us while we do not know who we are. Today our main danger is the worship of money, and the coins we use are our 'molten images'. The 'love of money is the root of all evil', so again St. Paul says:

> 'For I would not, brethren, that ye should be ignorant of this mystery, lest ye should be wise in your own conceits; that blindness in part is happened to Israel, until the fulness of the Gentiles be come in. And so all Israel shall be saved: as it is written, There shall come out of Sion the Deliverer, and shall turn away ungodliness from Jacob.'
>
> Romans, ch. 11, vs 25–26

A STUDY OF ISAIAH CHAPTER FORTY-TWO

Again, we return to Isaiah, who goes on to tell of the way that Israel has been robbed and spoiled:

> '. . . they are all of them snared in holes, and they are hid in prison houses: they are for a prey, and none delivereth; for a spoil, and none saith, Restore.'
>
> Isaiah, ch. 42, v. 22

When we come fully out of the world, all of British stock will be robbed of all they possess. We have seen it happen with the Arab world. We built the oil plants, and now they have taken them over and are charging us high prices for oil. It was the same in Africa. The local rulers drove out the British, but would not allow them to bring out their goods and money. All this is only the beginning. British firms who are sinking millions of pounds in opening large works abroad, and spoiling our own markets, are going to lose all when the nations go communist, and the Lord says:

> 'Who gave Jacob for a spoil, and Israel to the robbers? did not the LORD, he against whom we have sinned?'
>
> Isaiah, ch. 42, v. 24

We have asked for all we are going to get. If we had used all the money invested abroad in financing our own industries, we would have been economically strong today. Now we have to lose all the Gentile markets, but it will mean that we will be coming back to be safe in our Chambers when the world faces the terrible anger of the Lord. The Lord has given us to the robbers and spoilers, so that He can cover us in the day of wrath and give us more than we have ever lost in return. We will be a Kingdom of Priests, and an holy nation, and enjoy all the benefits of the new relationship with the Lord. All our enemies shall bow down before us, and we will rule over the heathen.

Chapter 12

JACOB'S TROUBLE

THERE seems very little doubt that we are now in the time of Jacob's trouble. We have written about this subject in the past, but now we can see just what it is, and how it will end. What is more, we can see the deliverance that it will bring.

> 'And these are the words that the LORD spake concerning Israel and concerning Judah. For thus saith the LORD; we have heard a voice of trembling, of fear, and not of peace. Ask ye now, and see whether a man doth travail with child? wherefore do I see every man with his hands on his loins, as a woman in travail, and all faces are turned into paleness?'
>
> Jeremiah, ch. 30, vs 4–6

Never before have the nations of the world held so many conferences about world security and peace and yet, with all the terrible weapons that are now in existence, the fear of war is always before the people. It is certain that a third world war would be far more devastating than the last. Thus, this verse is a true picture that will become more and more terrible as we go into the near future. The next verse is the one that is important to us as Israel.

> 'Alas! for that day is great, so that none is like it: it is even the time of Jacob's trouble; but he shall be saved out of it.'
>
> Jeremiah, ch. 30, v. 7

This verse can mean two things and we believe both. Jacob will be saved out of both the causes and the effects of his trouble.

The whole chapter must be read to find all the information which it contains, and this cannot all be dealt with in this chapter. Here we can deal only with the causes of and reasons for the trouble.

We (the British people) have turned away from our God and we no longer trust in the Lord, and so we have turned to other

JACOB'S TROUBLE

means of protection. As the Lord will not make Israel a conscript nation of slaves, He has given us our freedom, and we have used this freedom to turn even further away from Him. Thus, we have placed ourselves in great danger. We no longer love the Lord who has plainly said:

> 'Go and proclaim these words toward the north, and say, Return, thou backsliding Israel, saith the LORD . . . Turn, O backsliding children, saith the LORD; for I am married unto you . . .'
>
> Jeremiah, ch. 3, vs 12 and 14

The Lord claims to be the husband of Israel, but He accuses her of turning from Him and seeking many lovers. This is quite true, and can no longer be denied. We have gone after many lovers. As a matter of fact, from the standpoint of the Bible, we have gone to bed with many lovers! As we are a nation, our lovers must be nations, and so we can now list them. The first were the nations of U.N.O., when we put our faith in that godless organisation. Now there are over 100 member nations, all dedicated to peace and all arming up to the teeth! When the fear of Russian domination over Europe came into the picture we set up N.A.T.O. to keep her in eastern Europe and joined forces with many other nations, only now to find that the combined armies of all these nations are no match for Russia and the Warsaw Pact nations. Then we needed security in the Near East, so we set up S.E.A.T.O. and joined with yet other nations, only to find that they too have let us down. Then we felt that as we were just a weak off-shore island we must trust the Gentile nations for our food and trade, and so we joined the E.E.C. Now we don't know how many lovers we have got! All we do know is that they are very costly, and added to them, we have all the coloured nations (who we once sheltered, but who are now independent) which cost us more money and trouble than we can afford.

The churches are in the same boat, they have mostly turned away from God and are seeking unity with all kinds of religions, not only with the so-called Christian religions but with the heathen as well, maintaining that all serve the same God.

We turn to industry. Instead of supporting the firms which are doing well and making a profit, our people are turning to the political leaders who want nationalisation. The unions are seeking 'closed shop' provisions which means no man can work unless he joins the official union. In this way, the union leaders, most of whom are really communists, get control of the workers. Eventually they would like to link up with Russia.

Thus, our national leaders of Church, State and Industry are mating, or trying to mate, with every nation in the world! There is no need to pursue this brothel position any further other than to say that we are now so firmly in it that we have no way out. In fact, if it continued unchecked, finally we would have no say in our own home affairs.

We are now seeing the communist plot coming into the open in our own lands. All the Commonwealth nations are in the same domestic trouble as we are, so we are all in the same position. We are now told that there are a vast number of youths leaving school who cannot read, write, or do arithmetic, the basic things needed in later life. Communism is rampant among teachers, many of whom let their classes do just as they like. However, we now see the moderates are standing up to the communist pressure which is being put on them and the communistic shop stewards who have been controlling them are losing some power.

In a communist state it is essential that there is a large grade of men who are left illiterate and do all the rough work and who are unable to advance. These have to remain in the lowest grade. This appertains in a state that claims to have no class, but which has more grades than any other national system!

Then we have the people who seek to destroy our nation by infiltration, encouraging other nations to intermarry with the stock of Israel. This is given to us in the parable of the wheat and

JACOB'S TROUBLE

the tares. This parable is for the season before the final harvest of the world. It is seen to be true today and needs very little explanation.

> '. . . The kingdom of heaven is likened unto a man which sowed good seed in his field:'
>
> Matthew, ch. 13, v. 24

The sower is the Lord and the field is His own so it is the appointed place given to Israel to inhabit, and it was planted with good wheat.

> 'But while men slept, his enemy (Satan) came and sowed tares among the wheat, and went his way.'
>
> Matthew, ch. 13, v. 25

The parable then proceeds to tell of the effect of the sleep period of this nation that did not wake up to see the damage that was done to the crop until it was too late. We allowed Gentiles of all colours to come into this country and mix with the Israel stock in marriage. The churches have often been the worst of all offenders in this matter by encouraging such marriages. Now we can do nothing about it. In whatever direction we look we are beginning to see that there is no way out. Integration with all the other nations in every part of our national existence seems to be the only answer as far as people can see, but the Lord has the answer to the problem. In the parable, He says, let the wheat and tares grow together until the harvest and then the angels will remove the tares and leave the wheat in the field without contamination. In Jeremiah chapter thirty the Lord tells us that we cannot get out of our entanglements with the other nations. He says that this trouble is a correction in measure and that He will not leave us entirely unpunished, and so we are suffering for our waywardness.

> 'For thus saith the LORD. Thy bruise is incurable, and thy wound is grievous. There is none to plead thy cause, that thou mayest be bound up: thou hast no healing medicines. All thy lovers have forgotten thee; they seek thee not . . .'
>
> Jeremiah, ch. 30, vs 12–14

Here is God's answer. All the organisations will forsake us as they themselves break down and go into communism. They will have no pity for this nation, only hatred, because we will refuse to join with them and follow them in communism.

> '. . . for I have wounded thee with the wound of an enemy, with the chastisement of a cruel one, for the multitude of thine iniquity; because thy sins were increased . . . I have done these things unto thee.'
> Jeremiah, ch. 30, vs 14–15

The Lord says that by putting us in this position, which is the cause of our suffering, He will humble us. With Greece daggers drawn against Turkey, with Portugal in trouble and unstable, and with Italy already in the hands of the communists, N.A.T.O. must soon collapse. With our own trouble in Ulster, and because of our economic troubles, we have had to reduce our armies in Germany, and bring more forces home from the frontiers we are guarding. This will bring the defences in the West into a dangerous position, even more serious than they are now.

With the latest and most dangerous weapons in the hands of Russia and the U.S.A. all the weapons of the other nations could be rendered useless. Many years ago, in an article, we stated that the real reason for probing space was to find out if there was a more deadly and powerful military use for it than for anything we have on earth. Now we know that we were right. Both Russia and the U.S.A. have weapons, including H-bombs and laser beams that can be controlled from space, and directed to any part of the earth with more devastating effect than any of the latest weapons now being deployed on earth. We make this statement because of the verse in Revelation chapter thirteen:

> 'And he (the man over the beast system) doeth great wonders, so that he maketh fire come down from heaven on the earth in the sight of men,'
> Revelation, ch. 13, v. 13

The Bible says in this verse that the Russian leader uses something as a demonstration to the world to show that he can

JACOB'S TROUBLE 103

destroy any nation at will. This is one of the frightening weapons that will cause fear, as recorded in the passage we quoted at the beginning of this chapter.

With the will to resist in all the nations in the various organisations beginning to crumble, and with Russian influence overpowering them, they will all break down. Soon the English-speaking world will be left outside of all international organisations. The Lord is allowing us to get into this low state so that we will be freed from these other nations.

When the Common Market breaks up, France, Germany and Italy will go over to Russia as they are part of the ten toes of Daniel or the ten horns of Revelation. The countries of Denmark, Holland, Belgium and Luxembourg, although largely or partly Israel nations, will be taken over by Russia, leaving only Britain and Ireland free and we will see the glory of the Lord in what He has done. He has sent us into great trouble, but He will take us through it.

When we turn to Isaiah chapter forty-three we have a passage complementary to Jeremiah chapter thirty; both deal with Jacob's trouble and the result.

> 'But now thus saith the LORD that created thee, O Jacob, and he that formed thee, O Israel, Fear not: for I have redeemed thee, I have called thee by thy name; thou art mine. When thou passest through the waters, I will be with thee; and through the rivers, they shall not overflow thee: when thou walkest through the fire, thou shalt not be burned; neither shall the flame kindle upon thee.'
> Isaiah, ch. 43, vs 1–2

So despite all we have to suffer in the time of Jacob's trouble, we shall come through it unharmed. That this refers to the same trouble as Jeremiah chapter thirty is proved by the fact that both happen at the same time, that is, just before Israel withdraws into her Chambers, and into the safe keeping of the Lord. At this time the rest of the world will be going through the great tribulation (see Matthew, ch. 24, v. 21).

> 'Fear not: for I am with thee: I will bring thy seed from the east, and gather thee from the west; I will say to the north, Give up; and to the south, Keep not back: bring my sons from far, and my daughters from the ends of the earth; Even every one that is called by my name: for I have created him for my glory, I have formed him; yea, I have made him. Bring forth the blind people that have eyes, and the deaf that have ears.'
>
> Isaiah, ch. 43, vs 5–8

Now we turn once again to Jeremiah chapter thirty to show how much these two chapters match up.

> 'For I will restore health unto thee, and I will heal thee of thy wounds, saith the LORD; because they called thee an Outcast, saying, This is Zion, whom no man seeketh after.'
>
> Jeremiah, ch. 30, v. 17

This verse shows how all the lovers have left us completely alone.

> 'Thus saith the LORD; Behold, I will bring again the captivity of Jacob's tents, and have mercy on his dwellingplaces; and the city shall be builded upon her own heap, and the palace shall remain after the manner thereof.'
>
> Jeremiah, ch. 30, v. 18

This verse takes us from the time of Jacob's trouble, through the time when all nations turn against us when we come into our Chambers and into the Lord's security. Then it goes on through the time when the great tribulation is upon all the families of the earth to the Coming of the Lord, the last great battle, and to the time of the rebuilding of Jerusalem in the new age, when there will be one palace, the residence of the Lord Jesus Christ.

We now go on to verse twenty-two:

> 'And ye shall be my people, and I will be your God. Behold, the whirlwind of the LORD goeth forth with fury, a continuing whirlwind: it shall fall with pain upon the head of the wicked. The fierce anger of the LORD shall not return, until he have done it, and until he have performed the intents of his heart: in the latter days ye shall consider it.'
>
> Jeremiah, ch. 30, vs 22–24

JACOB'S TROUBLE

This punishment is not the same all the world over, but we see to which nations it is meted out if we turn back to verse sixteen:

> 'Therefore all they that devour thee shall be devoured; and all thine adversaries, every one of them, shall go into captivity; and they that spoil thee shall be a spoil, and all that prey upon thee will I give for a prey.'

Thus the punishments are graded by the Lord. He warned Israel not to take vengeance but to leave it to the Lord. The Lord says in referring to the last stage of Babylon:

> '. . . for it is the vengeance of the LORD: take vengeance upon her; as she hath done, do unto her.'
>
> Jeremiah, ch. 50, v. 15

Isaiah says:

> 'For it is the day of the LORD's vengeance, and the year of recompences for the controversy of Zion.'
>
> Isaiah, ch. 34, v. 8

> 'Say to them that are of a fearful heart, Be strong, fear not: behold, your God will come with vengeance, even God with a recompence; he will come and save you.'
>
> Isaiah, ch. 35, v. 4

In at least twenty other places in the Old Testament, which we cannot quote here, are similar references.

In conclusion, here is the present situation as I see it. Those people who are supporting the permissive society are over-reaching themselves, and their evil ideas are beginning to become nauseating to the people of the land, who are becoming aware of the evil and its danger. The workers are beginning to see that many of their leaders are out to destroy private industry, in favour of nationalisation, and that they do not care how many men are put out of work or how many works are closed down. The people are losing faith in all the political parties, and are beginning to get tired of having to live on promises. They are beginning to get fed up with rising prices and the fall in the pound.

These are all good signs and I feel fairly certain that soon we will be turning the corner and coming out of Jacob's trouble and beginning to seek the way back to the former days when we were a God-fearing nation. This would be the return to the Lord, and the beginning of the awakening of the nation to its identity. This of course will come slowly, but we pray that there will be a beginning, and we shall see the hearts of the people turning back to their God, the God of Israel.

Chapter 13

THE TWO PLANS – GOD'S AND SATAN'S

BEFORE we can proceed to see the line-up of the forces that will be engaged in the battle of the Lord, we must go back and recap a little of what we have already said.

When Adam fell he brought the whole of the Adamic race down with him, and Satan, by the will of the Lord, became the prince of this world. However, God retained for Himself the sacred line from Seth to Jacob, first one man in each generation, and then the twelve sons of Jacob.

When Israel came out of Egypt, the Lord separated the Israel people. From that day they became the people of the Kingdom of God, while all the rest of the nations remained as the kingdoms of this world under Satan, who rules them under the authority of God. Satan is still the prince of this world; but God appointed him to this position only until the time comes when He has trained His Israel people, and prepared them to take over the administration of the world under the Kingship of the Lord Jesus Christ.

Satan has always known that, when the time comes, and Israel is ready, he will be deposed. Because of this Satan has worked with might and main to secure for himself the nations of the world for ever, by trying to destroy Israel and the Church. He cannot think of a better plan than that of the Lord, which He has already made known in the Bible. In God's plan the Lord Jesus must return to the earth and into His Kingdom Israel; and then He must take over the other nations until all 'the kingdoms of this world are become the kingdoms of our Lord, and of his Christ' (Revelation, ch. 11, v. 15). This means therefore that all the nations of the world will be taken away from Satan, and they will become the kingdoms of God.

Satan is trying hard to bring all the nations of the world under one powerful nation, led by a man whom he has appointed and equipped. Satan also plans to rule over one great world wide power dominating all nations. We are told this at the time of the temptations of the Lord, when Satan showed Him all the nations of the world.

> 'And the devil, taking him up into an high mountain, shewed unto him all the kingdoms of the world in a moment of time. And the devil said unto him, All this power will I give thee, and the glory of them: for that is delivered unto me; and to whomsoever I will give it. If thou therefore wilt worship me, all shall be thine.'
>
> Luke, ch. 4, vs 5–7

Thus Satan tried to win over the Lord Jesus Christ by offering Him rulership over all the nations, without having to go to the cross and all its suffering. Satan would give Him everlasting control, and all he wanted in return was the continual worship of God the Son. This was his ambition from the time his pride took over. He was a mighty angel, but his aspiration was to be as God. In Isaiah, Satan says:

> 'I will ascend above the heights of the clouds; I will be like the most High.'
>
> Isaiah, ch. 14, v. 14

Satan wanted the worship of Jesus, thus separating Him from His Godhead, and causing Him to lose His holiness, and become a sinful man, but the trick, which caused Adam to fall, failed, and Satan's hope was lost. Now Satan's remaining hope is to get full control of Israel. So in Isaiah, Satan says:

> '. . . I will sit also upon the mount of the congregation, in the sides of the north.'
>
> Isaiah, ch. 14, v. 13

In the meantime Satan has tried every other means of getting the full control of the world. First he tried to corrupt all the people on the earth, and was under the impression that he had succeeded, but the Lord had reserved unto Himself one man.

THE TWO PLANS – GOD'S AND SATAN'S

So in His righteousness the Lord had to destroy the whole race in the flood, but saved Noah to carry on the Adamic family.

Then, Satan tried again. This time he tried to make one nation of all the people on the earth; to create a brotherhood of man, and so make that generation also disobey the Lord who had said:

> '. . . Be fruitful, and multiply, and replenish the earth.'
> Genesis, ch, 9, v. 1

This one disobedience would have put the whole of the human race under Satan, and this one act would have separated it from God. The Lord answered by giving them different tongues, so that they could not understand each other. The Lord divided them according to their families, giving each family a different language. Thus, the tribes came into being, and they separated and spread to the ends of the earth. Satan, now having failed twice, put into operation his third plan; to create a powerful nation that would subdue all the nations on the earth, with a powerful and evil leader, who would force all people to obey him, and look up to him as a god. In the case of Egypt, Assyria, Babylon, Medo-Persia, Greece, Rome, Spain, France and Germany, it often came near to succeeding. Egypt was broken by the Red Sea, then Assyria took over and was broken by Babylon, which in turn was broken by Medo-Persia, which fell to Greece, which finally gave way to Rome. Thus, the Lord defeated every attempt by Satan to form a world empire, by using another rising power to destroy the previous one.

Meanwhile, the Lord's plan was going forward. It has never changed. He has been steadily training Israel all through the ages: through bondage and freedom, through riches and poverty, through godliness and sin, through true worship and false, keeping the Law or breaking it, through experience in living, both as a nation and as individuals. The Lord is continuing the training in righteousness, which sometimes has proved very hard. The Lord appears hard and harsh, but behind it all, is His loving-kindness. At times Israel has gone so far from His Law that the nation should have been destroyed, but the Lord has loved Israel with an everlasting love, therefore with loving-kindness He has drawn her to Himself. Today we have gone far from our God, but from prophecy we know that He will bring us back to Himself. In fact, this is the last time that we will go astray.

When the Lord came to the earth He paid the price of all sin, past, present and future, and brought Israel into the New Covenant. Afterwards, one of the first things He did was to gather the tribes of Israel into the Islands. They were now God's battle axe and weapons of war and so they took up their new role. As they traversed the road across Europe, they weakened Rome so badly that it led to her downfall as a powerful nation, and ever since, Israel has been used by God for subduing the nations. It was Israel who defeated Satan's plans with Spain, France and Germany.

The time has now come (that is if we are as near to the Coming of the Lord as we think we are) for Israel to be drawn away from the world and return to God, and to enter into her Chambers and cease to be the Lord's battle axe. It is also the time when the kingdoms of the world are to be taken away from Satan, and his authority removed by God and given to the Lord Jesus Christ. Until this happens the Lord cannot return to the earth.

> 'I saw in the night visions, and, behold, one like the Son of man came with the clouds of heaven, and came to the Ancient of days, and they brought him near before him. And there was given him dominion, and glory, and a kingdom, that all people, nations, and languages, should serve him: his dominion is an everlasting dominion, which shall not pass away, and his kingdom that which shall not be destroyed.'
>
> Daniel, ch. 7, vs 13–14

That the transfer of the kingdoms from Satan to the Lord is just before His return, is plainly shown in Revelation.

> 'And the seventh angel sounded; and there were great voices in heaven, saying, The kingdoms of this world are become the kingdoms of our Lord, and of his Christ; and he shall reign for ever and ever.'
>
> Revelation, ch. 11, v. 15

That Satan will not give up his authority without a desperate struggle, a struggle which will make him inflame the nations of the world in anger against the take-over, is shown in the next verse:

> 'And the nations were angry, and thy wrath is come, and the time of the dead, that they should be judged, and that thou shouldest give reward unto thy servants the prophets, and to the saints, and them that fear thy name, small and great; and shouldest destroy them which destroy the earth.'
>
> Revelation, ch. 11, v. 18

Thus, for Satan and his angels, the great day of reckoning is near, and they will get no mercy and no quarter from the Lord, who will be truthful to them, for this is the time which the evil angels knew would come from the beginning and have dreaded it through the ages.

When the Lord was on earth, He went into the land of the Gadarenes, a Gentile people living on the borders of Judah; and there met a man who was possessed by many devils. When they saw Jesus, the evil spirits which possessed the man, fell at His feet and worshipped Him, saying:

> '. . . What have we to do with thee, Jesus, thou Son of God? art thou come hither to torment us before the time?'
>
> Matthew, ch. 8, v. 29

In the Gospel of St. Luke we get a fuller account of what was said:

> 'When he saw Jesus, he cried out, and fell down before him, and with a loud voice said, What have I to do with thee, Jesus, thou Son of God most high? I beseech thee, torment me not.'
>
> Luke, ch. 8, v. 28

These two statements show us plainly that the evil spirits knew full well that it was Jesus who would torment them sometime, but not then, and that they dreaded the day coming, when the Lord (at His Second Coming) would deal with them without mercy. They also claimed that the Lord could not touch them because they were possessing the body of a Gentile, and not an Israelite. This is the one case in which the Lord compromised with the evil spirits. He allowed them to go into the swine, instead of sending them straight back to the pit. If they dreaded the day then, how much more are they dreading it now that the time is so near!

We have already dealt with the fact that, before we can enter our Chambers and be absolutely safe while the judgments of the Lord are in the earth, all the Gentiles, whatever their colour and even the Israelites who have not accepted the Lord Jesus Christ will leave the Chambers. On the other hand, the Israel peoples will come in, including the people just the other side of the Channel, that is, the Israel stock of Norway, Holland, Luxembourg, Belgium and Denmark.

Here we must pause for a moment to clear up a point which is being raised by the modernists. They say that the two accounts about the devils meeting Jesus, which are quoted above, differ somewhat. The two Gospel writers, they note, both say different things. Therefore the modernists claim that they are unreliable, giving only hearsay evidence which does not correspond. The printers of the Bible made a great mistake when they headed the Gospels: 'according to St. Matthew', etc. What they should have used for the title was, 'The Gospel according to St. Matthew as inspired by the Holy Spirit', thus showing the harmony of all four.

It must be remembered that the Lord spent three years speaking and performing miracles. Each Gospel writer was given the necessary details to prove the case with which he was dealing. St. Matthew had to reveal the Lord Jesus Christ in His Kingship, so he starts off with the wise men who came to see the new born King. St. Mark had to deal with the Lord as the

THE TWO PLANS – GOD'S AND SATAN'S

servant, so he commenced with 'The beginning of the gospel of Jesus Christ, the Son of God; As it is written in the prophets,' and does not refer to the birth. St. Luke had to deal with the Lord's manhood, and so we have the humble birth and the visit of the shepherds. St. John in his turn had to deal with the Godhead of Jesus, so he begins with, 'In the beginning was the Word, and the Word was with God, and the Word was God.'

Each one used only a part of what happened, that seen from his own standpoint. Thus, Luke tells of the sinner who anointed the feet of the Lord, while John tells of Mary who anointed the feet of Jesus. It is easy to see, when comparisons are made, that the two events happened at different times, and in different places. This is just one example, there are plenty more. The Lord must have often spoken of the signs of the times, yet there is not one full report of what He said, only extracts. Now with that point cleared up we can go on with the events and talks of the Lord, and with the writings of the prophets regarding the scenes leading up to the great battle of the Lord.

It is not widely realised that, when we are entering into our Chambers, all evil spirits will be cast out from the place of safety. It is not stated in so many words, but it is a fact that can be seen.

We read in the book of Revelation chapter nine that the bottomless pit was opened, and all the devils in it were brought to the surface of the earth and were for a short time given freedom on the earth, where they attacked Israel and caused the death of the two witnesses in the Gentile world. Thus, they are the forces of Satan, used to drive Christianity out of the Gentile world, and thus to send the Gentiles into a communist and godless state, under Satanic control. We read that, once this has taken place, they will all be driven into the last and final Babylon and there in turn they will drive the nations in Babylon mad.

> 'For thus saith the LORD God of Israel unto me; Take the wine cup of this fury at my hand, and cause all the nations, to whom I send thee, to drink it. And they shall drink, and be moved, and be mad. . . .'
>
> Jeremiah, ch. 25, vs 15–16

Then follows a list of all the nations to whom the cup is given. Now we turn again to Revelation:

> 'And after these things I saw another angel come down from heaven, having great power; and the earth was lightened with his glory. And he cried mightily with a strong voice, saying, Babylon the great is fallen, is fallen, and is become the habitation of devils, and the hold of every foul spirit, and a cage of every unclean and hateful bird.'
>
> Revelation, ch. 18, vs 1–2

It is possible that this mighty angel is Michael who we are told was in charge of the angels who threw Satan and his angels (fallen angels) out of heaven, so that their place was no more found in heaven (see Revelation chapter twelve verses seven to ten). We say this may be the mighty angel because we read:

> 'And at that time shall Michael stand up, the great prince which standeth for the children of thy people: and there shall be a time of trouble, such as never was since there was a nation even to that same time: and at that time thy people shall be delivered, every one that shall be found written in the book.'
>
> Daniel, ch. 12, v. 1

It may be that your name is written in the book of the twelve tribes of Israel, but it is best to be safe, and to make sure that you have given yourself to the Lord Jesus, so that your name is written in the Lamb's book of life.

It is one thing to be in the national book under national salvation but another to be in the Church, the body of Christ, and therefore in the spiritual life of the nation. This is an important fact that many British Israel believers overlook; but it is plainly stated that we can enter by no other way than through the Lord Jesus Christ. We read in John chapter three, of Nicodemus who was a pharisee and therefore was of Israel stock. He was also a ruler of the Jews, and 'a Master of

Israel'(v. 10). When the soldiers went to arrest Jesus, instead of making the arrest, they reported back to the chief priests and pharisees and said, 'Never man spake like this man' (John, ch. 7, v. 46). It was Nicodemus (who came to Him by night) who faced them and said:

> 'Doth our law judge any man, before it hear him, and know what he doeth?'
>
> John, ch. 7, v. 51

It was Nicodemus, who with Joseph of Arimathea, lovingly buried the body of Jesus; and yet, despite all this, the Lord had said to him 'Ye must be born again' (John, ch. 3, v. 7). Just as it applied to Nicodemus, so it applies to us all, 'We must be born again!'

Chapter 14

THE BEAST – GOG, KING OF THE NORTH

> 'And I saw three unclean spirits like frogs come out of the mouth of the dragon, and out of the mouth of the beast, and out of the mouth of the false prophet. For they are the spirits of devils, working miracles, which go forth unto the kings of the earth and of the whole world, to gather them to the battle of that great day of God Almighty.'
> Revelation, ch. 16, vs 13–14

WE HAVE already dealt with the attack made by the dragon (Satan) (see Chapter 2, pp. 10–11) and shown that its object is to ensnare Britain with communism. This attack is gaining more and more in power. Only lately a bishop of the Church of England advocated that our nation go over to a communist government. This is the time of Jacob's trouble, but we are assured by God that we shall be delivered from it. We have also written about the false prophet (see Chapter 7, pp. 57–67). So now we come to the 'beast' and see what the Bible has to tell us about him.

We have already studied three of the four horses of Revelation chapter six (see Chapter 1, pp. 2–3, and Chapter 5, pp. 35–37) and shown that the white-clad rider of the first (white) horse is the Lord Jesus Christ. The white horse came fully into the world scene and began the preparations for the great and terrible day of the Lord in 1917 when Britain took control of the city of Jerusalem which marked the end of the time of the Gentiles (see Luke, ch. 21, v. 24). We have also seen that the second (red) horse and his rider symbolise the military power which seeks to dominate the nations. So we see that, following the establishment of ill-fated democracy, now nearly every change of government in the world is the result of military intervention, while an increasing number of countries

THE BEAST – GOG, KING OF THE NORTH

have military rulers or governments whose power depends on military enforcement. Even religious groups are using arms in mass attacks upon each other and governments are increasingly unable to restore law and order. We have also shown that the third (black) horse and his rider symbolise the wave of economic trouble that would come on the earth, and we know that this horse is now well into the picture for there is economic distress in nearly every land as everything, including food prices, gets out of balance.

Now finally, we come to the fourth horse with its rider. The rider is not yet in the saddle, but we are close enough to the time when he will be, to see clearly into the future as to what it will be like.

> 'And when he had opened the fourth seal, I heard the voice of the fourth beast say, Come and see. And I looked, and behold a pale horse: and his name that sat on him was Death, and Hell followed with him. And power was given unto them over the fourth part of the earth, to kill with sword, and with hunger, and with death, and with the beasts of the earth.'
>
> Revelation, ch. 6, vs 7–8

The meaning of this symbolism is fairly plain. This man will only have complete control over one quarter of the earth, but the system of his government will be world-wide in the Gentile world. This fact makes the whole picture clear. As we will show later in this chapter, this is the man who will be leading the armies of Russia and Europe against Palestine, and who will have his armies destroyed by the armies of the Lord. This is the most evil, satanic man in the world of evil men; the man who will deny that the true God exists, but who, as the greatest man on earth, will teach that he himself is supreme and that, therefore, he is God. His fall is shown in the book of Isaiah:

> 'Yet thou shalt be brought down to hell, to the sides of the pit. They that see thee shall narrowly look upon thee, and consider thee, saying, Is this the man that made the earth to tremble, that did shake kingdoms?'
>
> Isaiah, ch. 14, vs 15–16

In the book of the prophet Habakkuk we read:

> 'Yea also, because he transgresseth by wine, he is a proud man, neither keepeth at home, who enlargeth his desire as hell, and is as death, and cannot be satisfied, but gathereth unto him all nations, and heapeth unto him all people: . . . Woe to him that coveteth an evil covetousness to his house, that he may set his nest on high, that he may be delivered from the power of evil! . . . Thou art filled with shame for glory: drink thou also . . . the cup of the LORD's right hand shall be turned unto thee, and shameful spewing shall be on thy glory.'
>
> Habakkuk, ch. 2, vs 5, 9 and 16

This chapter tells us of this terrible man and of the graven image that he will set up, a 'molten image, and a teacher of lies,' (v. 18). He will say to the wooden image overlaid with gold and silver, 'Awake':

> 'Woe unto him that saith to the wood, Awake; to the dumb stone, Arise, it shall teach!'
>
> Habakkuk, ch. 2, v. 19

(We are told other things about this same terrible man in Daniel chapter eleven verses 30–45 and in Revelation chapter thirteen verses 11–18). However, Habakkuk chapter two also has two great messages as to the outcome of this evil man's wickedness:

> 'For the earth shall be filled with the knowledge of the glory of the LORD, as the waters cover the sea . . . But the LORD is in his holy temple: let all the earth keep silence before him.'
>
> Habakkuk, ch. 2, vs 14 and 20

Many of the world's dictators have planes ready to fly them to some place of safety should they fall from power, but this man has a nest in the heavens! This fact is supported by the statement in Obadiah:

> 'Though thou exalt thyself as the eagle, and though thou set thy nest among the stars, thence will I bring thee down, saith the LORD.'
>
> Obadiah, v. 4

THE BEAST – GOG, KING OF THE NORTH

The book of Obadiah, which is about a messenger that comes from God to stir up war against Edom, refers to the Idumeans. These Idumeans, who were descendants of Esau, were very powerful in the days of the Lord and had power in Palestine. Herod the Great was an Idumean. This is not stated in the Bible, but Josephus distinctly asserts that his immediate father (Antipater) was an Idumean who embraced Judaism as a religious belief.

The Idumeans continued to have a great influence over Jewry right up to 1917 when they became the masters of Russia and brought in communism. Since then they have worked to extend communism world-wide. Jeremiah chapter forty-nine, which deals with Edom (the Hebrew name of Idumea), states:

> '... though thou shouldest make thy nest as high as the eagle, I will bring thee down from thence, saith the LORD.'
> Jeremiah, ch. 49, v. 16

As noted above, Daniel chapter eleven contains a long passage concerning this man of mighty power who speaks great and marvellous things against the God of gods, and shall prosper till the indignation be accomplished. The Lord then says, 'for that that is determined shall be done' (v. 36). We then go to verse 42:

> 'He shall stretch forth his hand also upon the countries: and the land of Egypt shall not escape.'
> Daniel, ch. 11, v. 42

At the present moment we see Egypt trying hard to break the influence which Russia has had over her, and becoming more friendly with the West, but it is easy to see that this will not last. Our leaders are now stating that our friendship with the state of Israel does not prevent us being friendly with Egypt and supplying her with arms, although we know that Egypt's economy is so weak that she cannot pay for them. Be that as it may, we do know that Egypt will once again fall under the sway of Russia, until eventually she will be crushed into subjection and robbed of all she has.

> 'But he shall have power over the treasures of gold and of silver, and over all the precious things of Egypt: and the Libyans and Ethiopians shall be at his steps.'
>
> Daniel, ch. 11, v. 43

Continuing to the end of this chapter we read:

> 'But tidings out of the east and out of the north shall trouble him: therefore he shall go forth with great fury to destroy, and utterly to make away many. And he shall plant the tabernacles of his palace between the seas in the glorious holy mountain; yet he shall come to his end, and none shall help him.'
>
> Daniel, ch. 11, vs 44–45

It is impossible to say 'north-east' in Hebrew without using the idiom 'the north and the east', so 'tidings out of the east and out of the north' could be 'tidings out of the north-east'. If so, then this could mean that China and perhaps other eastern nations, will come up and try to invade the land of Israel before Russia can do so. We do know that China must play a part in the final scenes, for we read that the Lord will gather *all nations* against Jerusalem to battle in that day (Zechariah, ch. 14, v. 2). So the Lord states:

> 'Calling a ravenous bird from the east, the man that executeth my counsel from a far country: yea, I have spoken it, I will also bring it to pass; I have purposed it, I will also do it.'
>
> Isaiah, ch. 46, v. 11

Now we turn to Ezekiel chapters thirty-eight and thirty-nine; chapters which have long been called the 'Russian chapters'. The opening verses of both chapters are very much alike and are addressed to the same man:

> 'And the word of the LORD came unto me, saying, Son of man, set thy face against Gog, the land of Magog, the chief prince of Meshech and Tubal, and prophesy against him.'
>
> Ezekiel, ch. 38, vs. 1–2

THE BEAST – GOG, KING OF THE NORTH

We read in Genesis chapter ten, verse two, that Magog and Meshech were the sons of Japheth, and there is evidence to show that the Russians are of this same stock. So we note in passing, that eventually, and at the time of the great and terrible day of the Lord, the descendants of Japheth will be led by a Gentile-Jew, an Idumean, 'Gog' or 'the king of the north'. In verse three, God's message to this evil man is given:

> 'And say, Thus saith the Lord GOD; Behold, I am against thee, O Gog, the chief prince of Meshech and Tubal: And I will turn thee back, and put hooks into thy jaws, and I will bring thee forth, and all thine army . . .'
>
> Ezekiel, ch. 38, vs 3–4

Similarly, in Ezekiel chapter thirty-nine we read:

> 'Therefore, thou son of man, prophesy against Gog, and say, Thus saith the Lord GOD; Behold, I am against thee, O Gog, the chief prince of Meshech and Tubal: And I will turn thee back, and leave but the sixth part of thee, and will cause thee to come up from the north parts, and will bring thee upon the mountains of Israel:'
>
> Ezekiel, ch. 39, vs 1–2

The first two verses of chapter thirty-eight and the two verses of chapter thirty-nine must be read as two parts of one whole.

Thus, we know what will happen at and around Jerusalem, but what about events nearer home? We read in Revelation chapter twelve that after Satan has failed to subvert Israel in the Isles with the flood of lies (which is now taking place, and undoubtedly includes communism) he plans to attack her openly:

> 'And the dragon was wroth with the woman, and went to make war with the remnant of her seed, which keep the commandments of God, and have the testimony of Jesus Christ.'
>
> Revelation, ch. 12, v. 17

By this time we will be in our Chambers, while the whole of Europe will be under the power of Russia, with Gog in control of Russia, and Satan in control of Gog. The armies of Europe will be just the other side of the English Channel, ready and intending to attack us. However, what God has done in the past for His people Israel He will do again. In Isaiah we read that Judah had become very weak and Sennacherib, king of Assyria, sent an army against her. Sennacherib boasted that no nation had succeeded in war against him, in spite of prayers to their gods, and said that Hezekiah, king of Judah, would get no help from his God. Hezekiah laid the letter before the Lord, and prayed to the Lord. Soon the reply came to the king, and in Isaiah chapter thirty-seven we get the Lord's answer to, and about, Sennacherib:

> 'Because thy rage against me, and thy tumult, is come up into mine ears, therefore will I put my hook in thy nose, and my bridle in thy lips, and I will turn thee back by the way by which thou camest . . . Therefore thus saith the LORD concerning the king of Assyria, He shall not come into this city . . . By the way that he came, by the same shall he return, and shall not come into this city, saith the LORD. For I will defend this city to save it for mine own sake, and for my servant David's sake. Then the angel of the LORD went forth, and smote in the camp of the Assyrians a hundred and fourscore and five thousand: . . . So Sennacherib king of Assyria departed, and went and returned, and dwelt at Nineveh.'
>
> Isaiah, ch. 37, vs 29 and 33–37

The situation will be much the same again. Israel is weak and will have no army to match the combined forces of Europe, and Gog will be boasting against the Lord God of Israel. So we read:

> 'These have one mind, and shall give their power and strength unto the beast. These shall make war with the Lamb, and the Lamb shall overcome them . . .'
>
> Revelation, ch. 17, vs 13–14

As the text in Revelation chapter twelve shows, 'the dragon . . . went to make war'. However, we know that the attack against us will not even start. They are all set to invade and then the Lord puts hooks in their jaws and turns them back! What these hooks are, we do not know. Maybe it is the news from the north and the east that the eastern nations are ready to march into Palestine. This would appear to answer the passage, 'and will cause thee to come up from the north parts, and will bring thee upon the mountains of Israel.' (Ezekiel, ch. 39, v. 2). That is, Gog would move south into Palestine instead of invading Britain. The Lord could act in this way, but then we can often see several ways in which He could act. Frequently we are totally surprised when a prophesied event takes place; not at the event itself, but at the way in which God brings about its fulfilment. Indeed, after the fulfilment we find it hard to believe that we could ever have seen any other way before! So, we must await God's time to see what He will do, but meanwhile it is not wrong to speculate how He will achieve His purpose, always providing we do not seek to dictate to the Almighty how He must act, or become dogmatic in our predictions. So we can also see that the hooks could be the destruction of the whole of the Russian navy (the second plague – see chapter 6), or it could be the first plague, 'a noisome and grievous sore' that afflicts her armies (Revelation, ch. 16, v. 2). We can only trust the Lord that we will not be invaded, and wait and see how the Lord will prevent it.

However, it is certain that the land of Palestine will be invaded:

> 'Thou shalt ascend and come like a storm, thou shalt be like a cloud to cover the land, thou, and all thy bands, and many people with thee. Thus saith the Lord GOD; it shall also come to pass, that at the same time shall things come into thy mind, and thou shalt think an evil thought.'
>
> Ezekiel, ch. 38, vs 9–10

Maybe the evil thought is 'To take a spoil' (v. 12). Remember, the Lord is leading Russia and her allies to the place where He will meet them in His anger; and the place of the meeting is Jerusalem. This is where the spoil will be:

'And Judah also shall fight at Jerusalem; and the wealth of all the heathen round about shall be gathered together, gold, and silver, and apparel, in great abundance.'
Zechariah, ch. 14, v. 14

We also read that Jewry in Palestine will be placing all their trust in the great wealth which they will have gathered from the nations as they go communist. Using their knowledge of the counsels of high places they will know just when to remove their riches from the various nations, and will transfer them to Jerusalem. We also know that Jerusalem will not be bombed from the air. The air attack will be made in Lebanon, for we read that, just before the attack is made on Jerusalem,

'. . . he shall cut down the thickets of the forest with iron, and Lebanon shall fall by a mighty one.'
Isaiah, ch. 10, v. 34

We are also told from the Bible that this trust in their riches will not save Jewry in that day:

'Neither their silver nor their gold shall be able to deliver them in the day of the LORD's wrath; but the whole land shall be devoured by the fire of his jealousy: for he shall make even a speedy riddance of all them that dwell in the land.'
Zephaniah, ch. 1, v. 18

In Ezekiel Gog is addressed personally by the Lord:

'And thou shalt come up against my people of Israel, as a cloud to cover the land; it shall be in the latter days, and I will bring thee against my land, that the heathen may know me, when I shall be sanctified in thee, O Gog, before their eyes. Thus saith the Lord GOD; Art thou he of whom I have spoken in old time by my servants the prophets of Israel, which prophesied in those days many years that I would bring thee against them?'
Ezekiel, ch. 38, vs 16–17

We now come to the stage in our study where, while recognising the security of Israel in the Isles, we can see the opposing forces. Next we must consider the questions as to who forms the armies of Satan, and what comprises the armies of the Lord that go into the great battle? We know from the scriptures that the battle will be unlike any which has happened in the world so far, for in this battle the Lord Jesus Christ will be leading His army composed of human beings and angels for the first time. Against Him Satan will range all his evil forces, both human beings and fallen angels. So we see that the coming battle will be both spiritual and natural. We must go on to see what weapons the Lord will use in the battle. We know that the battle is the Lord's. So the Lord says of Russia (who is in control of the resurrected Babylon):

> 'I have laid a snare for thee, and thou art also taken, O Babylon, and thou wast not aware: thou art found, and also caught, because thou hast striven against the LORD. The LORD hath opened his armoury, and hath brought forth the weapons of his indignation: for this is the work of the Lord GOD of hosts in the land of the Chaldeans.'
>
> Jeremiah, ch. 50, vs 24–25

Chapter 15

THE TWO ARMIES – ANGELIC AND HUMAN

WE SAW in the last chapter how that the Lord is going to drive the evil angels of Satan into the communist nations and confine them there, so that they cannot get out. Thus, Satan's armies will combine his evil spirit forces as well as the human armies of all the godless nations. Among these human armies will be one drawn from Europe and led by Russia. South America will be allied with Russia, as will Egypt, the Libyans and the Ethiopians. Other opposing armed forces will come from the East led by China and Japan, while yet others will come from Arab Mohammedan nations led by Saudi Arabia. We will have to wait and see which of these sides the black African nations will be on. We know that they are being wooed by both Russia and China, both of whom are seeking to supply them with arms. Both Russia and China know that the arms will need spare parts, and both know that the side which wins the battle to supply arms now will soon have control over all central Africa. One thing is certain, the black African nations will be drawn into the great battle of the Lord.

Now we must look and see the forces which the Lord will use, and also, what are the weapons of His indignation. The Lord's armies will have to be both spiritual and human so as to meet the armies of Satan on both fronts. One thing is certain; the Lord Jesus Christ is both God and man. He is, therefore, supremely spiritual and human, and as such, He will be the leader of them both. On the other hand, Satan is a spirit who cannot become human. There is a gulf fixed by God that cannot be bridged between the life of an archangel (or angel) and the life of a man. Satan cannot enter into the womb of a woman, as Christ did. So,

THE TWO ARMIES – ANGELIC AND HUMAN

Satan will have to appoint a man, or men, to lead his earthly armies, and he will have to possess them, in the same way as he possessed Judas. On the night that the Lord Jesus was betrayed, we read in the Gospel, 'Then entered Satan into Judas' (Luke, ch. 22, v. 3).

We know that the arms of Russia and her allies are superior to ours in every way, but that need not worry us. The Lord is not going to meet the godless nations in their weakness, but in their strength, while the last generation of Israel will not take part in the battle, but will be safe in their Chambers (see Isaiah, ch. 26, vs 20–21, so often quoted in these chapters, and Isaiah, ch. 52, v. 12). When Israel enters into her Chambers, the days of her warfare will be over and she will no longer be God's 'battle axe and weapons of war' (Jeremiah, ch. 51. v. 20). She will be preparing to emerge as 'a royal priesthood, an holy nation' (I Peter, ch. 2, v. 9) and, according to God's Laws, the priesthood must not bear arms.

Before Israel became the nation of the Kingdom of God on earth the Lord kept evil in check by using the elements of nature. For example, in the time of Noah He used the Flood, and later in the day of Abraham He used fire and brimstone to destroy Sodom and Gomorrah. Finally, in the case of Egypt, He used the ten different plagues, all of which were natural with the exception of the last one by which He destroyed the firstborn of every family (as they had tried to destroy all the male babies of Israel in a former generation). After Egypt, with the establishment of the nation of Israel, God kept evil in check by using nation against nation, and by using Israel as His battle axe, only falling back on nature when Israel needed divine help, as in the days of the Spanish Armada. Once Israel is safe in her Chambers the Lord will once again use the elements of nature as His weapons. First of all we turn to Jeremiah chapter fifty; a chapter which is divided between the judgment of Babylon and the security of Israel. The following verses, which speak of Babylon, should be read together because the verses in between are concerning Israel:

> 'Cut off the sower from Babylon, and him that handleth the sickle in the time of harvest: . . . A sound of battle is in the land, and of great destruction. How is the hammer of the whole earth cut asunder and broken! how is Babylon become a desolation among the nations!'
> Jeremiah, ch. 50, vs 16 and 22–23

Here we have 'the hammer' and 'the sickle', the standard of Russia plainly shown to us. Continuing, we read:

> 'I have laid a snare for thee, and thou art also taken, O Babylon, and thou wast not aware: thou art found, and also caught, because thou hast striven against the LORD. The LORD hath opened his armoury, and hath brought forth the weapons of his indignation: for this is the work of the Lord GOD of hosts in the land of the Chaldeans.'
> Jeremiah, ch. 50, vs 24–25

Thus, the Lord will meet the armies of Satan with the weapons of nature: fire, earthquake, hail, thunder, plague, and famine; weapons against which Babylon has no answer. We read in Isaiah of the Lord's anger:

> 'The LORD shall go forth as a mighty man, he shall stir up jealousy (zeal) like a man of war: he shall cry, yea, roar; he shall prevail against his enemies. I have long time holden my peace; I have been still, and refrained myself: now will I cry like a travailing woman; I will destroy and devour at once. I will make waste mountains and hills, and dry up all their herbs; and I will make the rivers islands, and I will dry up the pools.'
> Isaiah, ch. 42, vs 13–15

It has always been a problem to many, as to what was meant by the first verses of this chapter:

> 'Behold my servant, whom I uphold; mine elect, in whom my soul delighteth; I have put my spirit upon him: he shall bring forth judgment to the Gentiles. He shall not cry, nor lift up, nor cause his voice to be heard in the street. A bruised reed shall he not break, and the smoking flax shall he not quench: he shall bring forth judgment unto truth. He shall not fail nor be discouraged, till he have set judgment in the earth: and the isles shall wait for his law.'
> Isaiah, ch. 42, vs 1–4

THE TWO ARMIES – ANGELIC AND HUMAN

That this chapter is all about the Lord Jesus Christ is agreed by all Bible students. However, He spent three and a half years in the streets, and He was speaking most of the time, and certainly lifted up His voice when addressing crowds of thousands (without the help of microphones as we have them today!). Yet this causes us no problems, because we understand that the passage quoted above does not refer to His ministry when on the earth, but to the two thousand years before He 'shall bring forth judgment unto truth.' This He will do at His Second Coming, and this is made plain by the statement lower down in the chapter, 'I have long time holden my peace . . . now will I cry' (v. 14). The intervening verses also make this quite plain. So we see that the Lord has waited for two thousand years, not condemning the world.

The question now facing us is, why does the Lord require an army of human beings? Surely He can cause fire to come down from heaven and consume all the armies of evil? The answer is that it is the beginning of the Lord's reign on the earth, when He will begin to rule over all the nations for one thousand years, bringing peace to the world and removing evil from the earth, so that the desert may blossom like the rose. This He must do in His manhood, as Jesus the Christ. The promise was given long ago that the Adamic race would have dominion after the defeat of Satan. The promise was also given that the Lord would take over the Throne of David and rule over the house of Israel for ever. Thus the Lord will claim the rulership because He is David's greater son. The promises made to Israel are for as long as the sun, moon, and stars continue, and so, Israel must share in that Kingdom of the Lord Jesus Christ during His thousand years reign. God needs His army of human beings not to fight in the battle, but to oversee His Law to all nations in the peace which will follow.

We know that the Lord must use the heavenly forces in the great battle, For He must not only destroy the power of Satan on earth, but, He must also enchain him and all his evil angels in 'the bottomless pit' for one thousand years:

> 'And I saw an angel come down from heaven, having the key of the bottomless pit and a great chain in his hand. And he laid hold on the dragon, that old serpent, which is the Devil, and Satan, and bound him a thousand years, And cast him into the bottomless pit, and shut him up, and set a seal upon him, that he should deceive the nations no more, till the thousand years should be fulfilled: and after that he must be loosed a little season. And I saw thrones, and they sat upon them, and judgment was given unto them: and I saw the souls of them that were beheaded for the witness of Jesus, and for the word of God, and which had not worshipped the beast, neither his image, neither had received his mark upon their foreheads, or in their hands; and they lived and reigned with Christ a thousand years. But the rest of the dead lived not again until the thousand years were finished. This is the first resurrection. Blessed and holy is he that hath part in the first resurrection: on such the second death hath no power, but they shall be priests of God and of Christ, and shall reign with him a thousand years.'
>
> Revelation, ch. 20, vs 1–6

From this passage alone it is plain to see that the Lord has been preparing His army from the day of Abel, whom the Lord called a righteous man (Matthew, ch. 23, v. 35). Its soldiers will include all the saints who were true to the Lord before the sons of Jacob were formed into a nation, and before the Church of the wilderness came into being. It will include all those members of the Church of Christ (to which the Church founded in the wilderness gave place) that is, all true believers in the Lord Jesus Christ who have received the new birth. All these died in the body, but their souls and spirits are waiting for this great resurrection. All these died in faith. The Lord told Daniel:

> 'But go thou thy way till the end be: for thou shalt rest, and stand in thy lot at the end of the days.'
>
> Daniel, ch. 12, v. 13

Isaiah believed the same great truth when, guided by the Holy Spirit, he wrote:

> 'Thy dead men shall live, together with my dead body shall they arise. Awake and sing, ye that dwell in dust: for thy dew is as the dew of herbs, and the earth shall cast out the dead.'
>
> Isaiah, ch. 26, v. 19

THE TWO ARMIES – ANGELIC AND HUMAN

The passage is referring to the time when Israel is in her Chambers, for the prophet goes on to say:

> 'Come, my people, enter thou into thy chambers, and shut thy doors about thee: hide thyself as it were for a little moment, until the indignation be overpast. For, behold, the LORD cometh out of his place to punish the inhabitants of the earth for their iniquity: the earth also shall disclose her blood, and shall no more cover her slain.'
>
> Isaiah, ch. 26, vs 20–21

David gave us his testimony when he said:

> 'For thou wilt not leave my soul in hell; neither wilt thou suffer thine Holy One to see corruption.'
>
> Psalm 16, v. 10

Job too was quite sure of the resurrection of the saints when he said:

> 'For I know that my redeemer liveth, and that he shall stand at the latter day upon the earth: And though after my skin worms destroy this body, yet in my flesh shall I see God: Whom I shall see for myself, and mine eyes shall behold, and not another; though my reins be consumed within me.'
>
> Job, ch. 19, vs 25–27

Before making this statement Job said (v. 23), 'Oh that my words were now written! oh that they were printed in a book!' His prayer was answered! The Holy Spirit inspired Job in what he said and caused it to be printed in the Book of books!

There is a contention as to where the dead are during the time of waiting. We know that their bodies are in the dust stage, but what has happened to their souls and spirits? On this subject I can only give what I believe, and why. Some believe in 'soul sleep' and give their reasons. Others believe that the dead are with the Lord. However, all believe that, waking or sleeping, they will all receive their bodies at the time of the Lord's return. This is too vast a subject to be dealt with here, and so I will give my belief in the next chapter.

Details concerning the Coming of the Lord are given in Psalm fifty:

> 'The mighty God, even the LORD hath spoken, and called the earth from the rising of the sun unto the going down thereof. Out of Zion, the perfection of beauty, God hath shined. Our God shall come, and shall not keep silence: a fire shall devour before him, and it shall be very tempestuous round about him. He shall call to the heavens from above, and to the earth, that he may judge his people. Gather my saints together unto me; those that have made a covenant with me by sacrifice. And the heavens shall declare his righteousness: for God is judge himself.'
>
> Psalm 50, vs 1–6

Whether we will have soul sleep, or soul consciousness is not a very important matter, although there is so much controversy about it. The main question which we have to decide is, have we made this covenant with God? Will we be in the First Resurrection and among those on whom 'the second death hath no power', or will we be in the Second Resurrection and have to face the great white throne and be judged according to our works? (see Revelation, ch. 20, vs 6 and 11–15).

> 'There is therefore now no condemnation to them which are in Christ Jesus, who walk not after the flesh, but after the Spirit.'
>
> Romans, ch. 8, v. 1

Chapter 16

THE COMING OF THE SAINTS

WE STATED in the last chapter that Satan will have two forces. One will be the armies of the communist world (and therefore human), while the other will comprise all the evil angels who will have been shut up in Babylon, and so will be ready for the battle. Thus, Satan's forces will be both human and angelic.

The Lord will also be in command of two armies with which He will destroy the armies of Satan. These armies must also be human and angelic, and so the angels of the Lord will come with Him into the battle:

> 'And to you who are troubled rest with us, when the Lord Jesus shall be revealed from heaven with his mighty angels, In flaming fire taking vengeance on them that know God, and that obey not the gospel of our Lord Jesus Christ.'
> II Thessalonians, ch. 1, vs 7–8

The human armies of the Lord will be all those in the B.C. age and in the A.D. age who worshipped Him in spirit and in truth.

The saints of the Old Testament firmly believed in the resurrection of the body. Job was very sure of this when he said:

> 'Oh that my words were now written! oh that they were printed in a book! That they were graven with an iron pen and lead in the rock for ever! For I know that my redeemer liveth, and that he shall stand at the latter day upon the earth: And though after my skin worms destroy this body, yet in my flesh shall I see God: Whom I shall see for myself, and mine eyes shall behold, and not another; though my reins (loins or kidneys) be consumed within me.'
> Job, ch. 19, vs 23–27

Isaiah gave the same great truth when he wrote:

> 'Thy dead men shall live, together with my dead body shall they arise. Awake and sing, ye that dwell in dust: for thy dew is as the dew of herbs, and the earth shall cast out the dead.'
> Isaiah, ch. 26, v. 19

We know that we are spirit, soul and body, but so far we have only named the body and so we now ask, what happens to the spirit and the soul when the body dies? The answer is that the spirit which gives life, and the soul which is in man, do not die but live on. The soul can die, but the spirit cannot die. It must return to God who gave it.

The departing of the soul is shown in the Bible to be the death of the body:

> 'And it came to pass, as her soul was in departing, *[for she died]* that she called his name Ben-oni (the son of my sorrow): but his father called him Benjamin (the son of the right hand). And Rachel died . . .'
>
> Genesis, ch. 35, vs 18–19

We are also told that if the soul returns to the body, then the body shall live. Elijah was sent to a widow during a period of famine, and was told to ask her for something to eat, and the widow shared what she thought was to be her last meal, for she had nothing left. However, the Lord renewed the food each time it was eaten, so that there was always one more meal for them. Later the young son of the widow died, and the widow rebuked the prophet:

> 'And he said unto her, Give me thy son. And he took him out of her bosom, and carried him up into a loft, where he abode, and laid him upon his own bed. And he cried unto the LORD, and said, O LORD my God, hast thou also brought evil upon the widow with whom I sojourn, by slaying her son? And he stretched himself upon the child three times, and cried unto the LORD, and said, O LORD my God, I pray thee, *let this child's soul come into him again.* And the LORD heard the voice of Elijah; *and the soul of the child came into him again, and he revived.*' [Our emphasis.]
>
> I Kings, ch. 17, vs 19–22

The Lord Himself confirmed the fact that the soul lives on after the death of the body when He said:

> 'And fear not them which kill the body, but are not able to kill the soul: but rather fear him which is able to destroy both soul and body in hell.'
>
> Matthew, ch. 10, v. 28

There are several words in the Greek and Hebrew which are all translated as 'hell' in the Authorised Version of the Bible. The word translated as 'hell' in this text from Matthew is 'gehenna', which means 'a place of punishment for the wicked'. Elsewhere in the Bible both 'sheol' and 'hades' are given as 'hell'. 'Sheol' is Hebrew and is given only in the Old Testament, while 'hades' is Greek and is given only in the New Testament. 'Sheol' and 'hades' both mean much the same, namely, the place of departed spirits, or the unseen world. Neither 'sheol' nor 'hades' means a place of punishment, but a place of *waiting* until the time of release or until the time of one of the two resurrections when the soul and spirit will be reunited with the risen body. The First Resurrection occurs at the end of the Christian age, and the Second Resurrection at the end of the Millennium:

> 'And I saw thrones, and they sat upon them, and judgment was given unto them: and I saw the souls of them that were beheaded for the witness of Jesus, and for the word of God, and which had not worshipped the beast, neither his image, neither had received his mark upon their foreheads, or in their hands; and they lived and reigned with Christ a thousand years. But the rest of the dead lived not again until the thousand years were finished. This is the first resurrection. Blessed and holy is he that hath part in the first resurrection: on such the second death hath no power, but they shall be priests of God and of Christ, and shall reign with him a thousand years.'
> Revelation, ch. 20, vs 4–6

The saints of the Old Testament time foresaw a time in hell (sheol) that would end for them with the Resurrection of the Lord. David saw this, when he said:

> 'Therefore did my heart rejoice, and my tongue was glad; moreover also my flesh shall rest in hope: Because thou wilt not leave my soul in *hell*, neither wilt thou suffer thine Holy One to see corruption.'
> Acts, ch. 2, vs 26–27

The word given as 'hell' in this verse is 'sheol' in Psalm sixteen (from which it is quoted in Acts) and 'hades' in Acts chapter two. This verse has a double fulfilment and refers both to David himself, and to the Lord Jesus Christ. David made a difference between his flesh and his soul in this verse. His body would rest in hope because his soul would not see corruption. The Lord rose from the grave on the third day, and His body was in the same condition as when He died – it had not seen corruption.

At the transfiguration of the Lord the three disciples that were with Him saw Him talking to Elijah and Moses. Now the fact that Elijah appeared in his body raised no problem as he did not die but was transported bodily into heaven. However, Moses died, and was buried, which did raise a problem, for the Bible says:

> 'Forasmuch then as the children are partakers of flesh and blood, he also himself likewise took part of the same; that through death he might destroy him that had the power of death, that is, the devil.'
>
> Hebrews, ch. 2, v. 14

The Lord had not yet died when Moses and Elijah appeared with Him on the Mount of Transfiguration, and so we read in the Epistle of Jude (v. 9):

> 'Yet Michael the archangel, when contending with the devil he disputed about the body of Moses, durst not bring against him a railing (injurious) accusation, but said, The Lord rebuke thee.'

Michael knew that Satan was justified in holding the body of Moses, so he told Satan that the Lord would rebuke him, and that caused Satan to let the body of Moses go.

When our Lord rose from the dead, Satan could no longer have any power over the bodies of men. The Lord took over full control of the bodies of His saints, when He broke the power of death.

> 'Thou hast ascended on high, thou hast led captivity captive: thou hast received gifts for men; yea, for the rebellious (Israel) also, that the LORD God might dwell among them. Blessed be the Lord, who daily loadeth us with benefits, even the God of our salvation. He that is our God is the God of salvation; and unto GOD the Lord belong the issues from death.'
>
> Psalm 68, vs 18–20

That He had this power over death from the moment of His Resurrection is proved by the fact given in these verses:

> 'For Christ also hath once suffered for sins, the just for the unjust, that he might bring us to God, being put to death in the flesh, but quickened by the Spirit: By which also he went and preached unto the spirits in prison.'
>
> I Peter, ch. 3, vs 18–19

The Lord was not heard by all the spirits in Hades, but as He told us Himself:

> 'Verily, verily, I say unto you, The hour is coming, and now is, when the dead shall hear the voice of the Son of God: and they that hear shall live . . . Marvel not at this: for the hour is coming, in the which all that are in the graves shall hear his voice, And shall come forth; they that have done good, unto the resurrection of life; and they that have done evil, unto the resurrection of damnation.'
>
> John, ch. 5, vs 25 and 28–29

Those that heard His voice at the time He spoke (as He said 'The hour is coming, *and now is*' – that is at His First Coming), certainly were liberated from the place of waiting and some even took up their bodies for a time:

> 'And the graves were opened; and many bodies of the saints which slept arose, And came out of the graves after his resurrection, and went into the holy city, and appeared unto many.'
>
> Matthew, ch. 27, vs 52–53

After His Resurrection the Lord halted on earth for a short time before He led captivity captive into heaven, while He contacted His disciples to tell them that He had risen from the dead. It was during this time that the risen saints were on the earth and so they had to have their bodies. Afterwards these bodies must have returned to the dust again, waiting for the First Resurrection, but what of their souls and spirits? They went with our Lord into heaven. Did He not say:

> 'In my Father's house are many mansions: if it were not so, I would have told you. I go to prepare a place for you. And if I go and prepare a place for you, I will come again, and receive you unto myself; that where I am, there ye may be also.'
>
> John, ch. 14, vs 2–3

Now, if we alter the word 'mansion' to 'house' (which is really the same thing) we get the understanding from St. Paul's writing:

> 'For we know that if our earthly house of this tabernacle were dissolved, we have a building of God, an house not made with hands, eternal in the heavens. For in this we groan, earnestly desiring to be clothed upon with our house which is from heaven: If so be that being clothed we shall not be found naked. For we that are in this tabernacle do groan, being burdened: not for that we would be unclothed, but clothed upon, that mortality might be swallowed up of life. Now he that hath wrought us for the selfsame thing is God, who also hath given unto us the earnest of the Spirit. Therefore we are always confident, knowing that, whilst we are at home in the body, we are absent from the Lord: *[For we walk by faith, not by sight:]* We are confident, I say, and willing rather to be absent from the body, and to be present with the Lord.'
>
> II Corinthians, ch. 5, vs 1–8

Just before he was facing yet another trial in the Roman courts, St. Paul also wrote:

> 'For me to live is Christ, and to die is gain. But if I live in the flesh, this is the fruit of my labour: yet what I shall choose I wot not. For I am in a strait betwixt two, having a desire to depart, and to be with Christ; which is far better: Nevertheless to abide in the flesh is more needful for you.'
>
> Philippians, ch. 1, vs 21–24

There are two questions which we now have to face. First, when we die do we meet our loved ones who died in the Lord? Second, after death do we have an awareness or a soul sleep? David was quite sure on the first point when he said:

> 'And he (David) said, While the child was yet alive, I fasted and wept: for I said, Who can tell whether GOD will be gracious to me, that the child may live? But now he is dead, wherefore should I fast? can I bring him back again? I shall go to him, but he shall not return to me.'
>
> II Samuel, ch. 12, vs 22–23

Now for the second point. Do we soul sleep after death until the Coming of the Lord, or, do we have an awareness of where we are and are soul conscious of what is going on in heaven? We have a perfect answer to this question in the book of the Revelation, chapter five. In this chapter we are told that there was a book, 'in the right hand of him that sat on the throne' (v. 1):

> 'And I saw a strong angel proclaiming with a loud voice, Who is worthy to open the book, and to loose the seals thereof? And no man in heaven, nor in earth, neither under the earth, was able to open the book, neither to look thereon.'
>
> Revelation, ch. 5, vs 2–3

The angels could not open the book. It had to be a human being. Notice that there were men in heaven, men alive on the earth, and dead men buried under the earth, none of whom could open the book. Clearly, therefore, there are *men* in heaven, so the question now revolves around whether they are conscious or not.

> 'And one of the elders saith unto me, Weep not: behold, the Lion of the tribe of Juda, the Root of David, hath prevailed to open the book, and to loose the seven seals thereof. And I beheld, and, lo, in the midst of the throne and of the four beasts, and in the midst of the elders, stood a Lamb as it had been slain, having seven horns and seven eyes, which are the seven Spirits of God sent forth into all the earth. And he came and took the book out of the right hand of him that sat upon the throne.'
>
> Revelation, ch. 5, vs 5–7

The next verse tells of the adoration of the twenty-four elders, and then we read:

> 'And they sung a new song, saying, Thou art worthy to take the book, and to open the seals thereof: for thou wast slain, and hast redeemed us to God by thy blood out of every kindred, and tongue, and people, and nation; And hast made us unto our God kings and priests: and we shall reign on the earth.'
>
> Revelation, ch. 5, vs 9–10

Then follows the adoration of the angels; but who are these that have been redeemed by the blood of the Lamb, and are in heaven, and yet are looking forward to the time when they shall reign on the earth? Surely they are the born again Christians, who had died up to that time, together with the saints of the Old

Testament who had been true worshippers of the Lord. The scene in heaven takes place after they had gone to heaven and before they return with the Lord to reign on the earth. They are not having a soul sleep, but they are fully aware of all that is going on in heaven. They are wide awake in spirit and soul, united together in the heavenly apparel which St. Paul mentioned in Second Corinthians.

We now turn to chapter six and see another scene in heaven:

> 'And when he had opened the fifth seal, I saw under the altar the souls of them that were slain for the word of God, and for the testimony which they held: And they cried with a loud voice, saying, How long, O Lord, holy and true, dost thou not judge and avenge our blood on them that dwell on the earth? And white robes were given unto every one of them; and it was said unto them, that they should rest yet for a little season, until their fellowservants also and their brethren, that should be killed as they were, should be fulfilled.'
>
> Revelation, ch. 6, vs 9–11

Like Daniel chapter eleven (vs 32–35) this refers to the final persecution of the Church, which we cannot deal with here. The main point to note here is that Revelation chapter six (v. 11) states that the souls under the altar were given 'white robes'. This is a certain sign that the time was ripe for the Lord to return to the earth at the close of the 'little (short) season'. In fact, it is the first preparation for the return of the Lord to the earth.

We now turn to a later scene, where the saints are dressed in 'white robes':

> 'After this I beheld, and, lo, a great multitude, which no man could number, of all nations, and kindreds, and people, and tongues, stood before the throne, and before the Lamb, clothed with white robes, and palms in their hands; And cried with a loud voice, saying, Salvation to our God which sitteth upon the throne, and unto the Lamb.'
>
> Revelation, ch. 7, vs 9–10

In this multitude, which no man could number, were all those who were killed for their faith, in the final persecution of the Church at the end of the Christian age, and had joined those who were already in heaven:

'And one of the elders answered, saying unto me, What are these which are arrayed in white robes? and whence came they? And I said unto him, Sir, thou knowest. And he said to me, These are they which came out of great tribulation, and have washed their robes, and made them white in the blood of the Lamb. Therefore are they before the throne of God, and serve him day and night in his temple: and he that sitteth on the throne shall dwell among them.'
Revelation, ch. 7, vs 13–15

We will have to leave the rest of this subject until the next chapter when we will consider the preparation for the last great battle of all time, the Coming of the Lord and the First Resurrection. However, in closing this chapter I would like to give a word of encouragement to those who are living, and who are born again of the Spirit of God, but somehow are afraid of death. This is a natural fear and a good one. If we did not fear death, then we would not trouble to look when we cross the road. The love of life makes us careful; but I write from what I know. Three times I have been in the valley of death, and believe me, there are some lovely flowers growing on the side of the valley, which take the fears away, and instead of fear comes the glorious hope, fast passing into reality:

'Thine eyes shall see the king in his beauty: they shall behold the land that is very far off.'
Isaiah, ch. 33, v. 17

Then you have that great moment, for the Lord says, 'I will come again, and receive you unto myself; that where I am, there ye may be also' (John, ch. 14, v. 3). Each believer makes the crossing of the river alone, but the Lord will see him safely to the other side.

A minister once watched by the bedside of his wife who the doctors had said would not live through the night, and twice the nurses thought she was dead, but she rallied and by the following day she had revived. Towards the evening she was well enough to say a few words, and the first words she said when she turned to her husband were, "I thought you always told us that when we were dying the Lord came to meet us!" He replied, "That is quite true. It is plainly stated by the Lord Jesus Himself." The amazing reply was, "Well, I was watching for Him all last night and He did not come," and her husband said, "No, my dear; He knew you were not going." What a glorious last night on earth that would have been, waiting to be with the Lord with no fear of death. All fear and sorrow were vanquished by her expectation of the immediate union with the Lord she loved.

Chapter 17

THE ARMIES OF THE LORD

WE HAVE already seen that the Lord's heavenly armies will be both angelic and human. The promise to the Adamic race was given by the Lord:

> 'What is man, that thou art mindful of him? and the son of man, that thou visitest him? For thou hast made him a little lower than the angels, and hast crowned him with glory and honour. Thou madest him to have dominion over the works of thy hands; thou hast put all things under his feet: All sheep and oxen, yea, and the beasts of the field; The fowl of the air, and the fish of the sea, and whatsoever passeth through the paths of the seas. O LORD our Lord, how excellent is thy name in all the earth!'
> Psalm 8, vs 4–9

This great statement regarding God's purpose in creating man is really a repeat of the following verses found in Genesis:

> 'And God said, Let us make man in our image, after our likeness: and let them have dominion over the fish of the sea, and over the fowl of the air, and over the cattle, and over all the earth, and over every creeping thing that creepeth upon the earth. So God created man in his own image, in the image of God created he him; male and female created he them. And God blessed them, and God said unto them, Be fruitful, and multiply, and replenish the earth, and subdue it: and have dominion over the fish of the sea, and over the fowl of the air, and over every living thing that moveth upon the earth.'
> Genesis, ch. 1, vs 26–28

We now turn to the New Testament and find that in Hebrews chapter two there is an almost verbatim repeat of Psalm eight, verses four to eight, and it is followed by:

> '... For in that he put all in subjection under him, he left nothing that is not put under him. *But now we see not yet all things put under him.* [Our emphasis.] But we see Jesus (the name of His humanity), who was made a little lower than the angels for the suffering of death,

crowned with glory and honour; that he by the grace of God should taste death for every man.'

Hebrews, ch. 2, vs 8–9

So the Promise is sure, and it is certain that the Adamic family will have dominion over the earth. However, it will only take place when the Lord Jesus is in control on earth. It is also certain that He can neither reign on earth as King on the Throne of David over Israel and the rest of the world, nor sit down on earth with the Apostles and eat and drink with them (and so keep the promise that he made to them on the night in which He was betrayed), either as Christ, the Spirit Being, or even as Jesus, a human man; but only as the Lord Jesus Christ – the man who is also God.

As the promise was made to the Adamic race, then they must rule with the Lord, and therefore, they must be represented at the great battle that will take place when that rulership begins to be enforced. As Christ, God the Son, He will be in charge of the angelic forces from heaven, which will subdue the evil spirit forces of Satan and imprison them in the bottomless pit. As Jesus, the Son of God, He will lead the army of humans from heaven, who will conquer and defeat the armies of the nations that will be in the battle against Jerusalem.

We saw in the last chapter that all the saints who have died are in heaven, praising the Lord, and looking forward to the time when they shall reign with Him 'on the earth' (see Revelation, ch. 5, vs 5–10). We also saw that they are to be given 'white raiment' so that they could come to the earth. This means that they cannot come back to the earth unclothed, with just their souls and spirits. They have to return as human beings, clothed in some bodily form.

> 'After this I beheld, and, lo, a great multitude, which no man could number, of all nations, and kindreds, and people, and tongues, stood before the throne, and before the Lamb, clothed with white robes, and palms in their hands; And cried with a loud voice, saying, Salvation to

our God which sitteth upon the throne, and unto the Lamb . . . And one of the elders answered, saying unto me, What are these which are arrayed in white robes? and whence came they? And I said unto him, Sir, thou knowest. And he said to me, These are they which came out of great tribulation, and have washed their robes, and made them white in the blood of the Lamb. Therefore are they before the throne of God, and serve him day and night in his temple: and he that sitteth on the throne shall dwell among them. They shall hunger no more, neither thirst any more; neither shall the sun light on them, nor any heat. For the Lamb which is in the midst of the throne shall feed them, and shall lead them unto living fountains of waters: and God shall wipe away all tears from their eyes.'

Revelation, ch. 7, vs 9–10 and 13–17

Now it is certain that, if the saints are 'before the throne', and the Lamb 'is in the midst of the throne', He cannot lead them to where they already are! So He must lead them away from the throne in heaven to where there are living waters. (There is the promise that the Lord is not going to take them again to be persecuted, or to hunger and thirst, and neither will they be left in the heat of the sun all day, as Our Lord was Himself.) He will usher in a time of peace, and therefore it says He will be leading them to the living waters. Psalm forty-six tells us of these waters which will be in existence when there is a New Jerusalem.

'There is a river, the streams whereof shall make glad the city of God . . .'

Psalm 46, v. 4

Moreover, in Psalm seventy-two, which tells of the reign of the Lord Jesus Christ, it says that:

'He shall have dominion also from sea to sea, and from the river unto the ends of the earth.'

Psalm 72, v. 8

Notice that 'the river' is singular. One river which shall go out to the ends of the earth! Ezekiel tells us about this river which will flow out from the Temple and become a great river which then divides into other rivers that go out to the ends of the earth (see Ezekiel, ch. 47, vs 1–12). Now turn with me to Revelation chapter twenty-two and read more about the same river:

> 'And he shewed me a pure river of water of life, clear as crystal, proceeding out of the throne of God and of the Lamb. In the midst of the street of it, and on either side of the river, was there the tree of life, which bare twelve manner of fruits, and yielded her fruit every month: and the leaves of the tree were for the healing of the nations.'
>
> Revelation, ch. 22, vs 1–2

That this takes place on earth is plainly stated in the first four verses of Revelation chapter twenty-one where again the promise is given that there will be no more tears or pain. It is true that this chapter is about the final Jerusalem that will come down to the earth after the one thousand years reign of the Lord (the Millennium), but it is also true that the temple and city described by Ezekiel has many similarities with the New Jerusalem, including the river of life. The subject of the thousand years reign would take up a whole chapter and cannot, therefore, be dealt with here.

Martha puts many of the leaders of the church, who do not believe in the return of the Lord to earth, to shame:

> 'Jesus saith unto her, Thy brother shall rise again. Martha saith unto him, I know that he shall rise again in the resurrection at the last day. Jesus said unto her, I am the resurrection, and the life: he that believeth in me, though he were dead, yet shall he live: And whosoever liveth and believeth in me shall never die. Believest thou this? She saith unto him, Yea, Lord: I believe that thou art the Christ, the Son of God, which should come into the world.'
>
> John, ch. 11, vs 23–27

The Lord Jesus said that generation after generation of believers would die, and would be brought back to life. However, the last generation that will be living at the time of the Lord's return will not die. Taken together these two statements lead us to the events of the First Resurrection which takes place before the Millennium. The events are given in several passages of the Bible and we have to line them up to try and get the full picture. We can get the main points, but some of the details are not plain yet.

THE ARMIES OF THE LORD

The first passage which we have to consider is found in Revelation chapter fourteen and it refers to some of that last generation who will die during the time of the great tribulation that will take place in the last few years of this present age:

> 'Here is the patience of the saints: here are they that keep the commandments of God, and the faith of Jesus. And I heard a voice from heaven saying unto me (John), Write, Blessed are the dead which die in the Lord from henceforth: Yea, saith the Spirit, that they may rest from their labours; and their works do follow them.'
>
> Revelation, ch. 14, vs 12–13

The previous verses dealt with the time when men will receive the mark of the beast in their heads or in their hands, but these have stood firm and borne witness in spite of the fierce opposition world-wide and are called home at death to return with the Lord at His appearing. These verses are followed by the First Coming of the Lord:

> 'And I looked, and behold a white cloud, and upon the cloud one sat like unto the Son of man, having on his head a golden crown, and in his hand a sharp sickle. And another angel came out of the temple, crying with a loud voice to him that sat on the cloud, Thrust in thy sickle, and reap: for the time is come for thee to reap; for the harvest of the earth is ripe. And he that sat on the cloud thrust in his sickle on the earth; and the earth was reaped.'
>
> Revelation, ch. 14, vs 14–16

Here we see the Lord Jesus Christ seated alone on a cloud, having left heaven and halted on the outskirts of the earth, waiting for the moment to come and the command from God the Father in the heavenly temple, for Him to complete His journey to the earth and to destroy the evil forces of Satan encamped around Jerusalem. We now turn to the words of our Lord in Matthew chapter twenty-four verse twenty-seven. In the previous verses He has been dealing with the false reports and alarms that will precede His Coming, and saying how easily many will be deceived by these reports. He says that some will come saying that they are Christ, and He warns us against them all, telling us to look for the great sign:

> 'For as the lightning cometh out of the east, and shineth even unto the west; so shall also the coming of the Son of man be. For wheresoever the carcase is, there will the eagles be gathered together.'
>
> Matthew, ch. 24, vs 27–28

'The carcase' is the spiritually dead body of Jewry in Palestine, and 'the eagles' are the ten nations of Europe.

> 'Immediately after the tribulation of those days shall the sun be darkened, and the moon shall not give her light, and the stars shall fall from heaven, and the powers of the heavens shall be shaken: And then shall appear the sign of the Son of man in heaven: and then shall all the tribes of the earth mourn, and they shall see the Son of man coming in the clouds of heaven with power and great glory. And he shall send his angels with a great sound of a trumpet, and they shall gather together his elect from the four winds, from one end of heaven to the other.'
>
> Matthew, ch. 24, vs 29–31

The words of the Lord give greater detail in Revelation:

> 'And I beheld when he had opened the sixth seal, and, lo, there was a great earthquake; and the sun became black as sackcloth of hair, and the moon became as blood; And the stars of heaven fell unto the earth, even as a fig tree casteth her untimely figs, when she is shaken of a mighty wind. And the heaven departed as a scroll when it is rolled together; and every mountain and island were moved out of their places. And the kings of the earth, and the great men, and the rich men, and the chief captains, and the mighty men, and every bondman, and every free man, hid themselves in the dens and in the rocks of the mountains; And said to the mountains and rocks, Fall on us, and hide us from the face of him that sitteth on the throne, and from the wrath of the Lamb: For the great day of his wrath is come; and who shall be able to stand?'
>
> Revelation, ch. 6, vs 12–17

On His way to the earth, the Lord must deal with the heavens and the evil therein:

> 'And you hath he quickened, who were dead in trespasses and sins; Wherein in time past ye walked according to the course of this world, (course – Hebrew, 'the course of things' or 'age') according to the prince of the power of the air, the spirit that now worketh in the children of disobedience:'
>
> Ephesians, ch. 2, vs 1–2

It is plain that Satan has power in the air. Therefore, the Lord deals with this power of Satan as He forces all the evil power and the evil angels from the heavens onto the earth, and confines them in Babylon. This activity means that the heavens and the stars must be shaken. (It is quite certain that the heavens and the stars must undergo a change of some kind to give the conditions on the earth during the Millennium which are foretold in the Scriptures, so that there is abundance of all plant growth to produce plenty of food for the population explosion that will occur during the thousand years of peace.)

> 'But I would not have you to be ignorant, brethren, concerning them which are asleep, that ye sorrow not, even as others which have no hope. For if we believe that Jesus died and rose again, even so them also which sleep in Jesus will God bring with him.'
> I Thessalonians, ch. 4, vs 13–14

Notice, although the saints' bodies are asleep, Satan no longer has any power over them, for they sleep in Jesus, even as we live in Jesus, covered by the blood of the Lamb. Their souls and spirits are with Him in heaven, and the care of their bodies is with Him while sleeping in the grave. Paul continues:

> 'For this we say unto you by the word of the Lord . . .'

Again we pause to see that St. Paul is making a great claim here, and he only makes this claim once more in the Bible. (We are told that he was called up to heaven to receive truths from the mouth of the risen Lord. The other occasion was when he was referring to the Breaking of Bread: 'For I have received of the Lord that which also I delivered unto you . . .' I Corinthians, ch. 11, v. 23.)

> 'For this we say unto you by the word of the Lord, that we which are alive and remain unto the coming of the Lord shall not prevent them which are asleep. For the Lord himself shall descend from heaven with a shout, with the voice of the archangel, and with the trump of God: and the dead in Christ shall rise first: Then we which are alive and remain shall be caught up together with them in the clouds, to meet the Lord in the air: and so shall we ever be with the Lord.'
> I Thessalonians, ch. 4, vs 15–17

Here then are plain statements of fact concerning these momentous events. Let us note the order:

(1) The Lord shall descend from heaven.
(2) When the Lord leaves the heavens He will bring the souls and the spirits of the saints with Him. So we read, 'we ... shall be caught up together with them.'
(3) There will be three great sounds when He comes: a shout, the voice of the archangel, and the trumpet of God.
(4) While the Lord will pause in the air (seated on a cloud – as we have read) the saints who come with Him from heaven will come right down to the earth to receive their earthly bodies at the First Resurrection.
(5) The saints who have come from heaven will then be joined with those saints on earth who believe on the Lord Jesus Christ and who have not died, thus forming the complete body of Christ (that is the Church of the ages).
(6) All these saints will then be caught up together to meet the Lord in the air, and from then on they will ever more be with Him as His body of which He is the Head.

This beautiful plan, revealed by the Lord, leaves one question unanswered. What will happen to the bodies of those saints who are living on earth at the time of the Lord's return, who, because they have not died, do not take part in the First Resurrection? How can they ascend to the Lord in the air? Not one of them will be perfect since they will all have their old sin-affected bodies. Clearly there is one more event which must also take place. It is an event which must be instantaneous in its operation, and it is recorded for us by St. Paul:

> 'Behold, I shew you a mystery; We shall not all sleep, but we shall all be changed, In a moment, in the twinkling of an eye, at the last trump: for the trumpet shall sound, and the dead shall be raised incorruptible, and we shall be changed.'
>
> I Corinthians, ch. 15, vs 51–52

THE ARMIES OF THE LORD

One change in the resurrection bodies is vital to know. The bodies which we have now were given organs to deal with the corruption caused by sin. These organs were part of the body of Adam in his perfection and only came into service when he became a sinner. However, the saints will never sin again in all eternity and these organs will be unnecessary and so the bodies will be changed to fit their eternal state. Thus we read:

> 'For this corruptible must put on incorruption, and this mortal must put on immortality. So when this corruptible shall have put on incorruption, and this mortal shall have put on immortality, then shall be brought to pass the saying that is written, Death is swallowed up in victory. O death, where is thy sting? O grave, where is thy victory? The sting of death is sin; and the strength of sin is the law. But thanks be to God, which giveth us the victory through our Lord Jesus Christ.'
> I Corinthians, ch. 15, vs 53–57

The one thing that stands out is that all these things happen at one and the same time. Thus, the change is at the last trump ('... at the last trump: ... and we shall be changed', I Corinthians, ch. 15, vs 51–52), while the Lord said that his angels 'shall gather together his elect' with 'a great sound of trumpet' (see Matthew, ch. 24, v. 31), and the apostle Paul explains that 'the trump of God' is the sign heralding the immediate resurrection of the dead in Christ (I Thessalonians, ch. 4, v. 16). So all three events, the gathering of the saints, the resurrection of the dead in Christ, and the change experienced by those saints alive at the time, are all heralded by the same trumpet blast.

We have noted that the Lord is seen sitting on a white cloud, and that the saints gather to meet the Lord 'in the clouds' and 'in the air'. So we see that the white cloud of Revelation chapter fourteen, verse fourteen, is the marshalling centre of the saints of the Lord – His human army. At the same time we must see that the voice of the archangel signifies the rallying call of the gathering of the angelic host to battle – the spiritual army of the Lord.

We read in Revelation that the archangel Michael is in charge of the angelic host of the Lord:

> 'And there was war in heaven: Michael and his angels fought against the dragon; and the dragon fought and his angels, And prevailed not; neither was their place found any more in heaven.'
>
> Revelation, ch. 12, vs 7–8

This happened in the past. Now we come right up to date and see the army standing for the defence of Israel in the Chambers:

> 'And at that time shall Michael stand up, the great prince which standeth for the children of thy people: and there shall be a time of trouble, such as never was since there was a nation even to that same time: and at that time thy people shall be delivered, every one that shall be found written in the book.'
>
> Daniel, ch. 12, v. 1

The term 'the children of thy people' includes all Israel, be they of Israel or of Judah. We know that the archangel Michael stands for the Lord in the defence of Israel for we are introduced to him fulfilling this role in Daniel chapter ten (read verses 12–21, especially verses 13 and 21). We must return to our subject, and so we now turn to Psalm fifty to get another picture of the united armies of the Lord:

> 'The mighty God, even the LORD, hath spoken, and called the earth from the rising of the sun unto the going down thereof. Out of Zion, the perfection of beauty, God hath shined. Our God shall come, and shall not keep silence (a reference to the great shout, etc.): a fire shall devour before him, and it shall be very tempestuous round about him. He shall call to the heavens from above, and to the earth, that he may judge his people (the word 'judge' here means 'to act as a magistrate'). Gather my saints together unto me; those that have made a covenant with me by sacrifice. And the heavens shall declare his righteousness: for God is judge himself.'
>
> Psalm 50, vs 1–6

The word 'judge' in this last verse means 'a discerner'.

When the Lord returns there will be those in Israel who are sharing in the national salvation, and others who are also in the Church having personal salvation as well, having made a covenant with the Lord through His sacrifice. This is brought out in the next verse:

'Hear, O my people, and I will speak; O Israel, and I will testify against thee: I am God, even thy God. I will not reprove thee for thy sacrifices or thy burnt offerings, to have been continually before me.'
>
> Psalm 50, vs 7–8

So God is not going to reprove the nation for their backslidings, but the Lord has to deal with the wicked in the nation, and so we read:

> 'Offer unto God thanksgiving; and pay thy vows unto the most High: And call upon me in the day of trouble: I will deliver thee, and thou shalt glorify me.'
>
> Psalm 50, vs 14–15

The next verses (vs 16–21) deal with the wicked in Israel, and then we read:

> 'Now consider this, ye that forget God, lest I tear you in pieces, and there be none to deliver. Whoso offereth praise glorifieth me: and to him that ordereth his conversation aright will I shew the salvation of God.'
>
> Psalm 50, vs 22–23

It therefore behoves each one of us to make sure that we will be safe in that day. Will you be ready to welcome the Lord when He comes to the world, or will you have to wait till the Second Resurrection some thousand years later? As we read in another place, Make your election sure!

> 'Of which salvation the prophets have inquired and searched diligently, who prophesied of the grace that should come unto you.'
>
> I Peter, ch. 1, v. 10

Chapter 18

CONDITIONS JUST BEFORE THE LORD'S RETURN SEEN FROM JERUSALEM

IN THE last chapter we saw the gathering of the saintly hosts of the Lord, and their being caught up in the air to meet the Lord in the clouds. We are now going to look at the gathering of the nations to the great battle, and so we are, as it were, going to stand in Jerusalem and see what is happening both in the city and the surrounding countries.

In Jerusalem every preparation is being made to resist the invaders. There is a man in charge: a man who claims to be the long awaited Messiah. He is being worshipped by, and lording himself over, the great body of Jews, both the true and false. These have been gathered from all over the world and feel proud to be under the leadership of this imposter who promises them both a mighty victory and to make them the rulers of the world.

For nearly two thousand years, at the feast of the Passover, Jewry has had a toast, 'This year here, next year in Jerusalem.' In 1917 that toast was partly fulfilled when Great Britain promised the Jews, in the Balfour Declaration, that they would have a national home in Palestine. Then in 1948 the Israeli nation came into being, and took over the major part of the country of Palestine and later in 1967 they took over the whole of the city including the Temple site. So the Jewish hopes for the coming of Messiah have become brighter and brighter. This expectation is being encouraged by the many Christians who say that Jewry is all Israel and a true stock of the people of God, thus helping Jewry to believe in their coming delusion. For Jewry will follow a man as the Messiah, and Christ, but he will be the wrong man and a false christ (he must be, as Jesus is the Christ and He has already come to His own but they received Him not). In fact, he will be the antichrist. Soon now that man will be revealed to the world. He will be able to prove that he is not only of the true Judah stock, but also of the line of David. Thus, Satan will be playing one of his last deceptions by setting up a rival to the true house of David in the Isles. There will be an attempt to set up a form of Judaism on the lines of the Mosaic Law and with the Levites, the priests, forming the government over the people, as they did after the time Jewry returned to Jerusalem from the captivity of Babylon until the city was destroyed in A.D. 70. Now they will be back in power.

Jewry will be placing their trust in this false messiah and also in the vast wealth which they have accumulated and stored in Jerusalem. This vast wealth is one reason for the prophesied invasion of Palestine by Russia, for she will want it both to carry on her world-wide dictatorship and for the invasion of the true Arab world which is to the south of Palestine (the king of the south). There are three passages in the Bible that tell us of this wealth, and they are all worth quoting:

> 'And Judah also shall fight at Jerusalem; and the wealth of all the heathen round about shall be gathered together, gold, and silver, and apparel, in great abundance.'
>
> Zechariah, ch. 14, v. 14

The next reference tells us that all this wealth, in which they are putting their trust, is only a false hope. It will not save them, but it will save the city from attacks by air and from being bombed into ruins.

> 'The great day of the LORD is near, it is near, and hasteth greatly, even the voice of the day of the LORD: the mighty man shall cry there bitterly. That day is a day of wrath, a day of trouble and distress, a day of wasteness and desolation, a day of darkness and gloominess, a day of clouds and thick darkness, A day of the trumpet and alarm against the fenced cities, and against the high towers. And I will bring distress upon men, that they shall walk like blind men, because they have sinned against the LORD: and their blood shall be poured out as dust,

and their flesh as the dung. Neither their silver nor their gold shall be able to deliver them in the day of the LORD's wrath; but the whole land shall be devoured by the fire of his jealousy: for he shall make even a speedy riddance of all them that dwell in the land.'

Zephaniah, ch. 1, vs 14–18

The previous verses state that:

'And it shall come to pass at that time, that I will search Jerusalem with candles, and punish the men that are settled on their lees (preserves): that say in their heart, The LORD will not do good, neither will he do evil. Therefore their goods shall become a booty, and their houses a desolation: they shall also build houses, but not inhabit them; and they shall plant vineyards, but not drink the wine thereof.'

Zephaniah, ch. 1, vs 12–13

This tells us that there must be an influx of population just before the Coming of the Lord, but the judgment will come very quickly after they have entered the land, so they will not be able to reap the fruits of their labour. Israel will settle down in a false state of security, totally unafraid of the states round about. This condition has not yet come, but it must be getting near. It may even come because the antichrist has drawn such a large following of men that they are in a numerically strong position and can ensure their own safety.

The Lord says of Russia and her allies:

'Thou shalt ascend and come like a storm, thou shalt be like a cloud to cover the land, thou, and all thy bands, and many people with thee. Thus saith the Lord GOD; It shall also come to pass, that at the same time shall things come into thy mind, and thou shalt think an evil thought: And thou shalt say, I will go up to the land of unwalled villages; I will go to them that are at rest, that dwell safely, all of them dwelling without walls, and having neither bars nor gates, To take a spoil, and to take a prey; to turn thine hand upon the desolate places that are now inhabited, and upon the people that are gathered out of the nations, which have gotten cattle and goods, that dwell in the midst of the land.'

Ezekiel, ch. 38, vs 9–12

First of all let us be sure the 'the land' in question is Palestine. Some writers are saying that the land referred to is the British

Isles. In fact, using the passage quoted next, one writer has even said that the battle of Armageddon will be fought in Kent!

> 'And thou shalt come from thy place out of the north parts, thou, and many people with thee, all of them riding upon horses, a great company, and a mighty army: And thou shalt come up against my people of Israel, as a cloud to cover the land; it shall be in the latter days, and I will bring thee *against my land,* that the heathen may know me, when I shall be sanctified in thee, O Gog, before their eyes.'
> Ezekiel, ch. 38, vs 15–16

(In the next chapter it states that Russia will lose five-sixths of her army and all her weapons in this invasion.)

It will be noticed that these Islands have never been the land claimed by the Lord as His own, yet the passage reads 'against my land'. These Islands are the 'appointed place' which the Lord gave to Israel after she left Palestine. It is greater Palestine which is 'my land'. Israel's land is the Islands where she shall 'move no more; neither shall the children of wickedness afflict them any more, as beforetime' (II Samuel, ch. 7, v. 10). These Islands have never been 'brought back from the sword;' (Ezekiel, ch. 38, v. 8). Notice that the Lord says that Gog would invade 'my land' from 'out of the north', that is, north of Palestine. If the British Isles were being invaded by Russia then the invasion would come from the east, and if Russia had control of all Europe (as she will have) then the invasion would come from the south. Then again we have the plain statement in Zechariah (ch. 14, v. 2): 'For I will gather all nations against Jerusalem to battle', and later in the same chapter it states that the Lord's feet 'shall stand in that day upon the Mount of Olives, which is before Jerusalem on the east.' That is the true geographical position of the Mount of Olives with respect to the City of Jerusalem. This to my mind, makes it quite certain that Jerusalem will be standing just where it has ever been when the prophecy is fulfilled, and the land of the invasion is Palestine.

The Russian leader will have the cream of all the armies of Europe with him when he invades Palestine. This will ensure that no European nation will revolt against him while he is invading the Middle East. We must also remember that these huge forces were first formed to attack and conquer Britain, after the communist plot to make Britain a communist country under Russian domination had failed.

> 'And the dragon was wroth with the woman, and went to make war with the remnant of her seed, which keep the commandments of God, and have the testimony of Jesus Christ.'
>
> Revelation, ch. 12, v. 17

However, the invasion of Britain will never be launched, but will be diverted to the Middle East. True Israel will be in her Chambers with her doors closed, crying aloud to all the nations that are being made godless under Russia the good news that the Lord will come and liberate them. This will be at a time when the nations are not only godless but have no hope of freedom or survival, and so we will be giving them hope of liberation from their oppressors.

> 'The LORD shall go forth as a mighty man, he shall stir up jealousy like a man of war: he shall cry, yea, roar; he shall prevail against his enemies.'
>
> Isaiah, ch. 42, v. 13

Russia will be in full control of all the nations north and south of the Mediterranean Sea. On the southern side, Morocco, Algeria, Tunisia and Libya. (Libya being the Greek word for all the regions of North Africa west of Egypt; the Hebrew word for the same region is 'Phut'):

> 'Persia, Ethiopia, and Libya with them; all of them with shield and helmet.'
>
> Ezekiel, ch. 38, v. 5

Please note that Persia is also named here, the Iran of today. Therefore, Iran will become allied with Russia. Ethiopia is the country that borders the Red Sea. Egypt of course has a Mediterranean coast and holds the Suez Canal:

CONDITIONS JUST BEFORE THE LORD'S RETURN

> 'He shall stretch forth his hand also upon the countries: and the land of Egypt shall not escape. But he shall have power over the treasures of gold and of silver, and over all the precious things of Egypt: and the Libyans and the Ethiopians shall be at his steps.'
> Daniel, ch. 11, vs 42–43

It is interesting to note that Egypt has been supplied with modern weapons of war from Russia and has lost them each time she has gone to war with Israel, so that Russia has had to equip her again. Now Egypt is trying to loosen the grip which Russia holds over her, but her debt is so great that she will find it impossible to break free. Russia will also be in control of all the European nations on the other side and so will have complete command of the Mediterranean Sea. The navies of the U.S.A. and Britain will find it closed to them. All the European nations on the north side are among the 'ten horn' nations (see Revelation, ch. 17, v. 12) that must come into judgment. In fact, the great earthquake which will take place at the Lord's Coming will cause havoc from one end of the Mediterranean Sea to the other, and several Mediterranean islands will disappear. So the Lord will see that we are right out of the Mediterranean scene before this happens. We can expect to see most of the nations bordering the Mediterranean go communist before the Coming of the Lord.

Russia will be free to use her large navy and its supporting ships to send all the heavy weapons of war across the Mediterranean Sea in preparation for her war, first with Israel and then with Saudi Arabia.

> 'And at the time of the end shall the king of the south push at *him*: and the king of the north shall come against *him* like a whirlwind, with chariots, and with horsemen, and with many ships; and he shall enter into the countries, and shall overflow and pass over.' [Our emphasis.]
> Daniel, ch. 11, v. 40

It is easy to understand that the prophets had to describe weapons of war in words understood at the time of writing, but we see that these can be modern weapons of war. This verse has been the source of much discussion over the years. The 'king of the north' is Russia, and the 'king of the south' is Saudi Arabia. Syria, Egypt and Lebanon are not true Arab countries and will all fall into the hands of Russia, together with the northern part of Palestine. This would give Russia the use of the port of Haifa, which is the nearest port to the Plain of Megiddo where Gog, the king of the north, assembles his weapons before the attack on Jerusalem. The main problem in this verse is the 'him'. Are there two sides one against the other, or is there a 'him' in between them? Is it just Arabia against Russia, or is the 'him' referred to, the leader of the Israelis? The verse can be taken both ways. We know that Russia will come with many ships while the Arabs have none, and so the meeting place must be in the region of Palestine. This leads us to see the position of the Arabs.

The Arabs are Moslems, the followers of the prophet Mohammed. There are various Moslem sects in the East, but the purest and the most powerful is centred in the Arabian peninsula. They believe in the prophets but teach that the three greatest are Mohammed, Abraham and Jesus. They believe in the virgin birth of Jesus but deny His Deity. They do not believe that He was crucified but that at the last moment the Lord God made Judas to look like Him and it was Judas who was hung. They believe that Jesus must return to be a great king, but that He will come to Mecca and not to Jerusalem. Their sacred book, the Koran, is based largely on the Old Testament. The Moslems are fatalists. That is, they believe in predestination, that one's life is predetermined before birth and one must conform to it. As they believe strongly in 'Allah, the One God', they will never accept communism which teaches that there is no God. Therefore, if communism is to sweep the world, it must conquer Arabia by force. This clears up the identity of the 'king of the south' and the 'king of the north' in Daniel chapter eleven and explains the need for such a mighty invading force with all the modern weapons of war. It could also explain why Russia may move quickly and withdraw her troops from Europe and so give up the idea of invading Britain.

> 'But tidings out of the east and out of the north shall trouble him: therefore he shall go forth with great fury to destroy.'
> Daniel, ch. 11, v. 44

This then is the overall picture. The Arabs are expecting the return of the prophet Jesus and so one of the false christs foretold in Matthew chapter twenty-four may be a great leader from the city of Mecca, a prince of Ishmaelite descent, and he could lead an army to try and stop the Russian invasion of the Middle East. He could also be against the Israelis, and so the verse quoted could have a dual meaning. At the same time the Jews are expecting the coming of Messiah (of the line of King David) to Palestine. When he arises he too will be a false christ. You can only imagine what could happen with several great leaders each claiming to be the saviour of mankind! Certainly it is easy to see how they would have to go to war to establish their claims. In the north, the atheists' humanist saviour, Gog, 'king of the north'; in Arabia, 'the king of the south', the prince of Islam; and in between them, the leader of the Jews, claiming to be the Christ.

Chapter 19

LAST ACTS OF THE PRESENT AGE

IN THIS last chapter we must continue to see all the events that will be taking place, leading to the final assembling of the nations and of the heavenly and evil hosts, from the standpoint of Jerusalem. We know that the nations are not free agents, but are being motivated by the Lord. However, as well as the compelling movements of the Lord, there are earthly reasons and these have to be considered.

The site of Solomon's Temple in Jerusalem is the only place where the Lord ordered and authorised that sacrifices be made. Since Jerusalem was destroyed in A.D. 70 by the Roman armies under Titus there have been no sacrifices under the Law of Moses. Nowhere in the Bible does the Lord say that, after the fall of Jerusalem at that time, another place would be given. Many religious Jews still look for the rebuilding of a Jewish temple on the original site of Solomon's Temple in Jerusalem and the resumption there of temple based worship. This is apparently impossible all the time the Mohammedan shrines stand on the site and are used for Moslem worship, as they still are today. The rebuilding of a Jewish temple on this site could be brought about by the destruction and demolition of the Moslem shrines, and this must be viewed as a real possibility. There may yet be another attack by the Arab world on the state of Israel, and this could lead to the bombing of Jerusalem and the destruction of the Mohammedan holy places including the Mosque of Omar which stands on the Temple site. Alternatively, an orthodox Jew, who is a fanatic, may place a bomb in the mosque (readers will recall that a fanatic tried to destroy a neighbouring mosque only a few years ago but was apprehended). This does not exhaust the possibilities in today's world of unrest. Of course, we do not have any direct statement in the Bible stating that any of these possibilities will definitely occur. However, it seems highly likely that something along these lines will take place because the Bible does appear to suggest that the Jews will build another temple on the sacred site before the Coming of the Lord. It may not be a completed structure, but one certainly covering the actual place of the sacrifices if it is built.

We have heard many reports saying that the Jews have all the building material ready for a new temple at Jerusalem, but we cannot get any direct evidence of this, and therefore, for the time being these reports must be discredited, or viewed with extreme caution. Of course the Jews have modified many buildings as synagogues through the years, and so the possibility cannot be ruled out that they might acquire the existing buildings and convert them for use as a temple. After all, the Mosque of Omar is an impressive structure, richly decorated, yet not contaminated in Jewish eyes by images and statues (such as pollute many Christian churches) because the Moslem religion forbids such things, as does the Law of the Old Testament. While we must wait to see what will happen, nevertheless, our reasons for suggesting that the temple at Jerusalem will be rebuilt or restarted are found in the Bible. For instance we read in Malachi chapter three, verse one:

'... and the Lord, whom ye seek, shall suddenly come to his temple ...'

In this prophecy the Lord is seen coming to judge the house of Levi and the house of Judah.

The Temple was the place where the high priest represented the people before the Lord and offered sacrifices for sin on his and their behalf. When the high priesthood was removed it was because the high priesthood was no longer an office on earth (although it continues in heaven in the person of the Lord Jesus

Christ, ordained a high priest for ever after the order of Melchizedek). In the account of the interview of the woman of Samaria with the Lord, we read that the woman says:

> '. . . Sir (Hebrew: Master), I perceive that thou art a prophet. Our fathers worshipped in this mountain; and ye say, that in Jerusalem is the place where men ought to worship. Jesus saith unto her, Woman, believe me, the hour cometh, when ye shall neither in this mountain, nor yet at Jerusalem, worship the Father. (This happened when Jerusalem was gutted.) Ye worship ye know not what: we know what we worship: for salvation is of the Jews. But the hour cometh, and now is, when the true worshippers shall worship the Father in spirit and in truth: for the Father seeketh such to worship him.'
>
> John, ch. 4, vs 19–23

The hour came to fulfilment when the veil of the Temple was 'rent in twain' (Matthew, ch. 27, v. 51), showing that sacrifices by the high priest were no longer acceptable to the Father, now that the Lord Himself was paying the full price of sin.

The priesthood that served in the Temple were of the family of Aaron; just one family of the tribe of Levi. The Aaronic priesthood went out of Bible history and prophecy when the Lord died. There is no mention of them in the prophecy relating to the coming age.

Apart from the descendants of Aaron, the rest of the tribe of Levi could not offer sacrifices to the Lord. They were the servants of the Lord in the synagogue to offer prayers to the Lord and the civil servants to teach His Law and administer it to the people. The tribe of Levi does have a place in the age to come when the Lord reigns on the earth, but we cannot go into that here. We are told:

> 'Let no man deceive you by any means: for that day (the return of the Lord) shall not come, except there come a falling away first, and that man of sin be revealed, the son of perdition; Who opposeth and exalteth himself above all that is called God, or that is worshipped; so that he as God sitteth in the temple of God, shewing himself that he is God.'
>
> II Thessalonians, ch. 2, vs 3–4

For these reasons we believe that the Temple will be rebuilt in Jerusalem. We have no reason to believe that sacrifices will be offered as this man will be of the tribe of Judah and the house of David, and he will claim to be the long awaited Messiah to the Jewish people. He will gather true Judah to himself. He will be bombastic and boastful and defiant against all the communist nations. He will gather to himself most of the gold and silver of the heathen communist world, and this means that Russia will be after the wealth of Judah, and so will China. When he sees all the nations assembled against him he will claim to have the power to order the heavenly hosts to come to his defence and he will call on the angels of heaven to come to his aid. To this end there will be a great day of prayer and fasting and the calling of a solemn assembly. It is really the Lord who orders it, and it will lead to the Lord's going into action:

> 'Blow the trumpet in Zion, sanctify a fast, call a solemn assembly: Gather the people, sanctify the congregation, assemble the elders, gather the children, and those that suck the breasts: let the bridegroom go forth to his chamber, and the bride out of her closet. Let the priests, the ministers of the LORD, weep between the porch and the altar, and let them say, Spare thy people O LORD, and give not thine heritage to reproach, that the heathen should rule over them: wherefore should they say among the people, Where is their God? Then will the LORD be jealous for his land, and pity his people.'
>
> Joel, ch. 2, vs 15–18

At the same time, Israel, who will be safe in their Chambers, will be praying for the remnant in Palestine. Thus all Jacob will be praying for the Lord to go to the defence of His city:

> 'For thus saith the LORD; Sing with gladness for Jacob, and shout among the chief of the nations: publish ye, praise ye, and say, O LORD, save thy people, the remnant of Israel.'
>
> Jeremiah, ch. 31, v. 7

We get some idea of what this deluded, Satan-inspired person will be like when we realise that he will be ruling with a seemingly hypnotic power which will enable him to mesmerise the whole of the Jewish people into believing what he thoroughly believes himself in his self-deception, that he really is the long awaited Messiah. This deception of himself and of the people must be very strong when we consider that they will stand defiant when the world's greatest armies all appear at their borders. The Bible gives us a terrible picture of the event. It almost seems as if the Lord will harden their hearts as He did with Pharaoh so long ago. The event is seen in several chapters of the Bible, and we have to read them all to get the picture.

> 'Behold, I will make Jerusalem a cup of trembling unto all the people round about, when they shall be in the siege both against Judah and against Jerusalem. And in that day will I make Jerusalem a burdensome stone for all people: all that burden themselves with it shall be cut in pieces, though all the people of the earth be gathered together against it.'
>
> Zechariah, ch. 12, vs 2–3

This antichrist cannot be the high priest of the temple, as he must stake his claim to be of the house of Judah and of the house of David. Thus, the governors of Judah will be the Levitical priesthood, acting under this deluded head.

The question now arises as to the position of the house of Israel in that day. They have no part in this 'cup of trembling'. We held the cup (Jerusalem) from 1917 to 1948, and then we gave up Jerusalem and the Israelis took it over, thus fulfilling the prophecy of Isaiah chapter fifty-one, verse twenty-one, to Israel who is 'afflicted, and drunken, but not with wine' (see also Isaiah, ch. 29, especially verse 9).

> 'Therefore hear now this, thou afflicted, and drunken, but not with wine: Thus saith thy Lord the LORD, and thy God that pleadeth the cause of his people, Behold, I have taken out of thine hand the cup of trembling, even the dregs of the cup of my fury; thou shalt no more drink it again: But I will put it into the hand of them that afflict thee;

which have said to thy soul, Bow down, that we may go over: and thou hast laid thy body as the ground, and as the street, to them that went over.'
Isaiah, ch. 51, vs 21–23

This prophecy is given in greater detail in Ezekiel chapter twenty-three in which the Lord tells us of the sins of the people:

'Son of man, there were two women, the daughters of one mother (Sarah): . . . And the names of them were Aholah the elder, and Aholibah her sister: and they were mine, and they bare sons and daughters. Thus were their names; Samaria is Aholah (His tent, or tabernacle), and Jerusalem Aholibah (My tabernacle in her).'
Ezekiel, ch. 23, vs 2 and 4

Thus, we have both Israel and Judah, for Samaria was the capital city of Israel and Jerusalem was the capital of Judah. For the next twenty-seven verses the chapter recounts the sins of the two nations against the Lord, and then in verse thirty-two we read:

'Thus saith the Lord GOD; Thou (Judah) shalt drink of thy sister's cup deep and large: thou shalt be laughed to scorn and had in derision; it containeth much. Thou shalt be filled with drunkenness and sorrow, with the cup of astonishment and desolation, with the cup of thy sister Samaria.'
Ezekiel, ch. 23, vs 32–33

This cup is found mentioned in various other places in the Bible, for example:

'Upon the wicked he shall rain snares, fire and brimstone, and an horrible tempest: this shall be the portion of their cup.'
Psalm 11, v. 6

'For in the hand of the LORD there is a cup, and the wine is red; it is full of mixture; and he poureth out of the same: but the dregs thereof, all the wicked of the earth shall wring them out, and drink them.'
Psalm 75, v. 8

We now turn to Jeremiah:

'For thus saith the LORD God of Israel unto me; Take the wine cup of this fury at my hand, and cause all the nations, to whom I send thee, to drink it. And they shall drink, and be moved, and be mad, because of the sword that I will send among them. Then took I the cup at the LORD's hand, and made all the nations to drink, unto whom the LORD had sent me:'

Jeremiah, ch. 25, vs 15–17

Then follows the list of all the nations who will partake of the cup, starting with Jerusalem and Egypt and then twenty-three other nations by name, and many people with them. Then we read:

'Therefore thou shalt say unto them, Thus saith the LORD of hosts, the God of Israel; Drink ye, and be drunken, and spue, and fall, and rise no more, because of the sword which I will send among you. And it shall be, if they refuse to take the cup at thine hand to drink, then shalt thou say unto them, Thus saith the LORD of hosts; Ye shall certainly drink.'

Jeremiah, ch. 25, vs 27–28

Now for just one more reference from the Old Testament we turn to Zephaniah:

'Therefore wait ye upon me, saith the LORD, until the day that I rise up to the prey: for my determination is to gather the nations, that I may assemble the kingdoms, to pour upon them mine indignation, even all my fierce anger: for all the earth shall be devoured with the fire of my jealousy.' (The Hebrew word given as jealousy also means zeal, that is a strong feeling of love or anger.)

Zephaniah, ch. 3, v. 8

The reason for the confederate nations going to war with the Jews in Israel is because they are defiant of the communist world. Proud of their way of life, they will not bend. It is also the first step to the conquest of Arabia, to force the Moslem world into communism. Both China and Russia must get power over Arabia if they are to go on to dominate the communist world. However, these communist nations do not know that the Lord God of Israel is using their deception and their plans for His own ends. It is His way of gathering all the nations to meet, not so much with Israel in Palestine as to meet Him and to come into judgment. All the nations of the world will be taking military action against the people in Palestine, except the true

LAST ACTS OF THE PRESENT AGE

Israel people (now safely in their Chambers) led by Britain and the U.S.A. It is true that Russia will have control of the Mediterranean Sea and so we will not be able to go to her help, but we will be planning to invade from the Red Sea; to try and get there to help the people. However, the Russian advance on Jerusalem from the north will be too fast for us, and besides, it is the Lord's will that we will not get there in time. For this information we have to go to Isaiah:

> 'Woe to the land shadowing with wings, which is beyond the rivers of Ethiopia:'
>
> Isaiah, ch. 18, v. 1

(*N.B.* The Hebrew word translated 'Woe' can also mean 'Ho', and should be read as 'Ho' in this case.)

The shadowing wings signifies protection. The phrase is used in this way six times in the Psalms, but we will only quote one example here:

> 'Because thou hast been my help, therefore in the shadow of thy wings will I rejoice.'
>
> Psalm 63, v. 7

Ethiopia is the name used by the Greeks and the Romans for the land called Cush by the Hebrews, after the descendants of Cush the son of Ham who occupied that country to the south of Egypt. Therefore the land which has the protection of the Lord is below the great rivers that divide Africa. When on my visit to South Africa I was shown the three rivers from the air; it made the prophecy easy to understand. At present, all the nations of north and central Africa are under native rule while only two countries beyond the rivers are under white rule, namely, Rhodesia and South Africa! The next verse shows great activity:

> 'That sendeth ambassadors by the sea, even in vessels of bulrushes upon the waters, saying, Go, ye swift messengers, to a nation scattered and peeled, to a people terrible from their beginning hitherto; a nation meted out and trodden down, whose land the rivers have spoiled!'
>
> Isaiah, ch. 18, v. 2

If the first word of Isaiah chapter eighteen, verse one, really should be translated 'Woe', then verse two is also correctly translated and means what it says, but if this first word really means 'Ho' (a call to the nations) then the second verse must also mean something else. In fact, the translators were unclear as to the translation of verse two and so they gave an alternative rendering of it in the margin, which fits better with 'Ho' than with 'Woe'. This other, and correct, translation is:

> 'That sendeth ambassadors by the sea, even in vessels of bulrushes upon the waters, saying, Go ye swift messengers, to a nation outspread and polished, to a people terrible from their beginning hitherto; a nation that meteth out, and treadeth down . . .'
>
> Isaiah, ch. 18, v. 2

This now makes sense. It is the true Israel block of nations that are using southern Africa as a centre for preparing a great expeditionary force, assembled by sea from various parts of the Israel block. South Africa is the only spot suitable for Britain, Canada, the U.S.A., Australia and New Zealand, to assemble an armed force to go to the help of Judah in Palestine as the hosts of evil prepare to invade Palestine from the north, the east, the west, and the south.

Verses three to six are addressed to the nations of the world and sum up the fate that will come upon them. Then in the last verse we read:

> 'In that time shall the present be brought unto the LORD of hosts of a people outspread and polished, and from a people terrible from their beginning hitherto; a nation meted out and trodden under foot, whose land the rivers have spoiled (cleaved), to the place of the name of the LORD of hosts, the mount Zion.'
>
> Isaiah, ch. 18, v. 7

It is interesting to read these verses from the Revised Standard Version:

> 'At that time gifts will be brought to the LORD of hosts from a people tall and smooth, from a people feared near and far, a nation mighty and conquering, whose land the rivers divide, to Mount Zion, the place of the name of the LORD of hosts.'

This is Israel of the northern house bringing themselves as a present to the Lord with a mighty force, too late to be involved in the battle of the Lord, but ready to clear up the land according to Ezekiel chapter thirty-eight. This present to the Lord is also referred to in Zephaniah:

> 'From beyond the rivers of Ethiopia my suppliants, even the daughter of my dispersed, shall bring mine offering.'
> Zephaniah, ch. 3, v. 10

This is a perfect link with Isaiah chapter eighteen and shows the mercy of the Lord, in that He has prepared for the swift cleansing of the land of Palestine after its destruction.

That the word 'polished' is the more suitable translation and refers to Israel is to be found in Isaiah:

> 'And he hath made my mouth like a sharp sword; in the shadow of his hand hath he hid me, and made me a *polished* shaft; in his quiver hath he hid me; And said unto me, *Thou art my servant, O Israel, in whom I will be glorified.*' [Our emphasis.]
> Isaiah, ch. 49, vs 2–3

All the people who say we are down and out and passing away like all the other empires before us, know nothing of the plans of the Lord. Over three thousand years ago the Lord formed Israel with the one objective, to glorify His Holy Name, and it is His sovereign will that we do so, in spite of our waywardness. So He will bring us back to Himself in our affliction, and we will obey Him willingly and proudly as His servant nation, inspired by the Holy Spirit.

GLOSSARY

(Explanatory notes about Bible prophecy terms used in this book)

Antichrist(s) – Satan is anti-God and hence anti-Christ, for Christ is God. Moreover, all and any who serve Satan and his purposes are also antichrist. There are, therefore, many antichrists (see I John, ch. 2, v. 18). Antichrist is defined as, 'he that denieth that Jesus is the Christ', and, 'He . . . that denieth the Father and the Son' (see I John, ch. 2, v. 22). Thus, all those who have Judaism as their religion, since the death, resurrection and ascension of the Lord Jesus Christ, are antichrist, for they claim to have the Father, but deny the Son. 'Whosoever denieth the Son, the same hath not the Father' (I John, ch. 2, v. 23). Antichrist also includes those who deny 'the Father and the Son' and hence includes all atheists.

There have been many who are antichrist, and some by virtue of their concerted persecution of anything which is God's, during the A.D. era, deserve to be known as an antichrist. However, it is clearly stated that one particular individual should appear who would be 'antichrist', ('ye have heard that antichrist shall come' – I John, ch. 2, v. 18), and this individual is identified as the antichrist. In this book the antichrist is shown to be the leader of Jewry in Palestine, who will claim to be the Messiah, and hence Christ and God. He will be a descendant of Judah, and David, and will achieve power just before the Second Coming of the Lord Jesus Christ, who will destroy him at His Coming. *The* antichrist is also known as '*the* false prophet', and '*the* son of perdition', and '*that* man of sin', for in his delusion he will be Satan-possessed. (See also in this glossary 'the false prophet'.)

Babylon – This name is used often in the book of Revelation (e.g. see Revelation, ch. 14, v. 8, ch. 16, v. 19, ch. 17, v. 5 and ch. 18, vs 2 and 10). It refers to the succession of empires wielding political, economic, military and religious power in the Gentile world, beginning with the literal Babylonian Empire under King Nebuchadnezzar (see Daniel, ch. 2, especially verses 36–43), and continuing into the later forms of the Roman Empire. It is also used to refer collectively to the final resurrected forms of these empires, all allied with Russia, and voluntarily obeying Gog and his beastly system of government.

Beast, the – Often in Bible prophecy, beasts symbolise empires. For example, see Daniel chapter seven verse seventeen. As such empires were often absolute dictatorships, the beast represents at one and the same time, both the empire and its ruler. Thus in Daniel chapter two verse thirty-eight, 'Thou art this head of gold.' The head of gold was both the whole Babylonian Empire and King Nebuchadnezzar, its ruler. This type of symbolism continues in the New Testament (see Revelation, ch. 13, vs 1–4), where the beast is distinct from the head, and continues with several different successive heads. The beast system of empires will continue until the Second Coming of the Lord Jesus Christ. Immediately prior to that event there will be a final world empire. As a whole the empire is the beast, yet as with Nebuchadnezzar, its ruler, by virtue of his absolute power (he is the head), is also the beast. The last manifestation of the beast system is the Russian Empire (called Leviathan in Job chapter forty-one).

This duality of system and individual is clearly shown in the wording of Revelation, ch. 13, vs 11–18. The Russian Empire and allied nations (the beast), will consist of Russia, Persia, Ethiopia, Libya (see Ezekiel, ch. 38, v. 5) and all the nations of eastern and western continental Europe, including many at present free who will yet 'give their power and strength unto the beast' (Revelation, ch. 17, v. 13). The ruler of this power bloc (the chief prince of Meshech and Tubal) is also 'the beast personified'. 'Gog', 'the king of the north' – also in this glossary – will live up to his title 'the beast'.

Chambers – This term is used in this book in the sense of Isaiah, ch. 26, v. 20, 'Come, my people, enter thou into thy chambers'. It refers to those geographical locations (mostly islands) appointed by God to the nations of Israel (see Deuteronomy, ch. 32, vs 8–9) and especially that safe land promised by God to David for Israel's future earthly habitation outside of the land of Palestine (see II Samuel, ch. 7, v. 10). Thus, it includes the British Isles (see 'the Isles' in this glossary) and many of the other Israel nations (see 'Israel' in this glossary) including Canada, Australia, New Zealand, Ireland, the U.S.A., and parts of southern Africa. The 'Chambers' are the only lands where Christianity will survive immediately prior to the Second Coming of the Lord, and will be safe from invasion by all ungodly forces and from most of the plagues of judgment poured out by God upon the rest of the world (see Isaiah, ch. 26, vs 20–21).

Dragon – A name given to Satan, used in the book of Revelation (see Revelation, ch. 12, vs 7–9, and ch. 20, vs 1–3). It is Satan (the dragon) who gives his earthly power to 'the beast' (Revelation, ch. 13, v. 4), and in return receives the worship of men, which he has craved since his first rebellion against God, and his attempt to be as God (see Isaiah, ch. 14, vs 12–14).

GLOSSARY

False Jew(s) – see Jews, False.

False prophet – Throughout history there have been many false prophets, as the Bible foretold (see Matthew, ch. 24, v. 24); the so-called prophet Mohammed, founder of Islam, being a notable example. However, the final individual referred to in Revelation as 'the false prophet' is identified in this book as an individual ruling over Judah and Levi in Palestine at the time of the Lord's return, who claims to be the Prophet promised in Deuteronomy and the Messiah. As the Lord Jesus Christ was the Prophet promised in Deuteronomy and the Messiah, it follows that this other man is an imposter and a 'false prophet'. The false prophet is also referred to as 'that man of sin' and 'the son of perdition' (II Thessalonians, ch. 2, v. 3).

Gog – The individual who will be the dictator ruling Russia 'the chief prince of Meshech (Moscow) and Tubal (Tobolsk)' and many other nations at the time of the Lord's Second Coming (see Ezekiel, ch. 38, vs 2–5). He is also referred to in the Bible as 'the king of the north' (see Daniel, ch. 11, v. 40). (*N.B.* There have been several kings of the north during prophetic history, but Gog will be the final one. Moscow is almost exactly due north of Jerusalem.) He is also referred to as 'the beast' (see Revelation, ch. 19, v. 19). Like 'the king of the north' there have been several 'beasts' during history, but Gog will be the last to correctly fulfil this unenviable role as exactly foretold in Bible prophecy.

He it is who will lead the major force invading Palestine from the north (see Ezekiel, ch. 38, vs 15–16) and fighting in Jerusalem when the Lord Jesus Christ returns (see Zechariah, ch. 14, vs 1–4).

Gentile Jew(s) – see Jews, False.

Isles – The term 'the Isles' and 'the Islands' in this book refers to the British Isles and Ireland, which are identified as 'the Isles' occupied by Israel late in history, and where Isaiah repeatedly addresses them in his prophecy (e.g. Isaiah, ch. 41, vs 1 and 8–9; Isaiah, ch. 42, v. 4; Isaiah, ch. 49, vs 1–3). These Islands are one of the Chambers of 'places of safety' appointed for Israel by God, in fact, they are the main such place, since they contain the Throne of David (the Royal House).

(See also in this glossary: Chambers and Place of safety.)

Islands – see Isles.

Israel – Throughout this book Israel is clearly distinguished from the Jews and is used to refer to that group of nations (see Genesis, ch. 35, v. 11 and Genesis, ch. 48, v. 19), the recipients of, and exhibitors of the covenants and promises made by God to the seed of Abraham, Isaac and Jacob (whose name was changed to Israel) and the birthright given to the seed of Joseph and Ephraim. These nations are identified as the Anglo-Saxon-Celtic nations and peoples of Great Britain, Eire, the U.S.A., Canada, Australia, New Zealand, and southern Africa, together with their kin in Scandinavia and other coast lands of north-west Europe and elsewhere.

Israel's chambers – see Chambers.

Jew(s) – A distinction is made throughout this book between the Jews and Israel. The Jews are most correctly defined as the descendants of those Israelites (mostly of the tribes of Judah and Levi) who lived in the kingdom of Judah prior to its termination in 586 B.C. (by King Nebuchadnezzar of Babylon) and especially of those who returned after the exile and lived in Palestine at the time of the Lord's death and resurrection. On the other hand, Israel is taken as being mainly formed of the descendants of the Israelites who lived in the northern kingdom of Israel (terminated in 721 B.C. by King Sargon II of Assyria) led by the tribe of Joseph. Thus, the terms are used in accordance with the prophecy of Ezekiel, ch. 37, vs 15–22; the 'Jews' being 'Judah, and . . . the children of Israel his companions', and 'Israel' being 'Joseph, . . . and *all* the house of Israel his companions' (see verse 16). The reunion of Israel and Judah is anticipated as foretold (see verses 21–22) but has not yet occurred.

Jew(s), False – During history many who were not Israelites by race adopted Judaism as their religion, often under duress (for example see Esther, ch. 8, v. 17) and their descendants are not included in the fulfilment of the promises made to Judah in the Bible. Such are termed False Jew(s) or Gentile Jew(s) in this book.

Jew(s), True – In this book the term 'true Jew(s)' refers to individuals descended from Jacob/Israel, whose ancestors were subjects of the southern kingdom of Judah, some of whom returned after the exile and lived in Palestine during our Lord's earthly ministry (see 'Jew(s)' and 'False Jew(s)' in this glossary). True Jews have been scattered in many, if not all nations since the time of the exile, and to this day there are more true Jews living outside of Palestine than in the Israeli state. Thus, for the purpose of this book 'true Jew' is racially defined and does not include those of non-Israelite descent who have adopted Judaism as their religion. However, it does include a large number of those of Israelite blood who have no religion and are atheists or agnostics. The true Jews are those in whom the promises and statements made concerning Judah and Levi in the Bible will be confirmed or fulfilled.

Kings of the east – As with all directions in Bible prophecy the reference point is the Temple site in the city of Jerusalem in Palestine. Consequently,

GLOSSARY

'the kings of the east' (a term used only once in the Bible in Revelation, ch. 16, v. 12) must refer to rulers of lands east of Palestine. It is taken to refer to China, and perhaps to Japan, in this book, although it may refer to other rulers also. These rulers will also be involved in the invasions of Palestine occurring immediately prior to the Second Coming of the Lord. The phrase 'But tidings out of the *east* and out of the north' (Daniel, ch. 11, v. 44) probably refers to the activities of 'the kings of the east'.

King of the north – As with all directions in Bible prophecy the reference point is the Temple site in the city of Jerusalem in Palestine. Consequently, 'the king of the north' is a ruler of a land north of Jerusalem. Several rulers have filled this role during history in fulfilment of the prophecy of Daniel chapter eleven, but the final 'king of the north' will be the dictator of Russia who will invade Palestine from the north just prior to the Lord's Second Coming (see Daniel, ch. 11, vs 40–45). (*N.B.* Moscow is almost exactly due north of Jerusalem.) See also 'Gog' in this glossary.

King of the south – As with all directions in Bible prophecy the reference point is the Temple site in the city of Jerusalem in Palestine. Consequently, 'the king of the south' is a ruler of a land south of Jerusalem. Several rulers have fulfilled this role during history including the rulers of Egypt. However, the final 'king of the south' will be the ruler of Saudi Arabia, a descendant of Ishmael the half-brother of Isaac. He will be an ardent and warlike follower of Mohammed, and will lead an invasion of Palestine by Islamic forces at the same time as 'the king of the north' (see Daniel, ch. 11, v. 40) immediately prior to the Second Coming of the Lord Jesus Christ.

Man of Sin – see Antichrist(s) and False prophet.

Millennium – The term 'the Millennium' as such is not used in the Bible. However, it is used by Bible students as a form of shorthand to refer to the thousand year period, following the Second Coming of Christ, and between the First and Second Resurrections, during which Satan will be enchained in 'the bottomless pit' and the Lord Jesus Christ will reign *on earth* from Jerusalem (see Revelation, ch. 20).

Place of safety – A place of safety for the habitation of Israel outside of the land of Palestine was promised to King David by Nathan the prophet as recorded in II Samuel, ch. 7, v. 10: 'Moreover I will appoint a place for my people Israel, and will plant them, that they may dwell in a place of their own, and move no more; neither shall the children of wickedness afflict them any more, as beforetime.' This place is identified as the British Isles (see 'Isles' in this glossary) where Israel (see 'Israel' in this glossary) dwells in safety. The place of safety is one of the Chambers appointed by God for the Israel nations (see 'Chambers' in this glossary).

Second Coming – Although Christ visited this earth (as God, the second Person of the Trinity) on many occasions during ancient times, He did not come as a man and to stay until His incarnation when he was named Jesus (which means Saviour) as a baby. At His death and resurrection He fulfilled the promise in His Name, becoming THE SAVIOUR, the Lord Jesus Christ and then He ascended to His Father in heaven. This period of His human life on earth, although not so named in the Bible, is often referred to by Bible students as the First Coming of Christ, and it did more to change and shape subsequent history than any life before it. Now we await His return, that is, the return of the man, in physical form, to live here on earth (not just to visit). Such a return is repeatedly promised in the Bible, not least by the 'men' on the mount of Olives, at His ascension (Acts, ch. 1, vs 9–11): 'And when he (Jesus) had spoken these things, while they beheld, he was taken up; and a cloud received him out of their sight. And while they looked stedfastly toward heaven as he went up, behold, two men stood by them in white apparel; Which also said, Ye men of Galilee, why stand ye gazing up into heaven? this same Jesus *(the man),* which is taken up from you into heaven, shall so come in like manner as ye have seen him go into heaven.' Similarly (Zechariah, ch. 14, vs 3–4), 'Then shall the LORD go forth, and fight against those nations, as when he fought in the day of battle. And *his feet* shall stand in that day upon the mount of Olives, which is before Jerusalem on the east . . .' This return, eagerly awaited by the faithful, is referred to by Bible students as the Second Coming of the Lord.

Son of Perdition – see Antichrist(s) and False prophet.

Stone Kingdom – This expression uses the symbolism of Daniel (ch. 2, vs 34–35) to refer to God's Kingdom which will destroy all other earthly kingdoms and cover the whole earth. Thus, 'and the stone . . . became a great mountain, and filled the whole earth' (v. 35), or in the interpretation (v. 44) 'in the days of these kings shall the God of heaven set up a kingdom, which shall never be destroyed: . . . it shall break in pieces and consume all these kingdoms, and it shall stand for ever.' This prophecy will find its final great fulfilment in the Kingdom of God on earth which Christ will establish during the millennium following His second coming. However, it has had another ongoing fulfilment in the history of the Israel kingdom, reigned over by the Davidic Throne, which is Great Britain. The stone kingdom in Daniel chapter two does what Jacob was promised in Isaiah, ch. 41, vs 14–16: 'Fear not, thou worm Jacob, and ye men of Israel; I will help thee, saith the LORD, and thy redeemer, the Holy One of Israel. Behold, I will make thee a new sharp threshing instrument having teeth: thou shalt thresh the mountains, and beat them small, and shalt make the hills as chaff. *Thou* (Israel) shalt fan them, and the wind shall carry them away, and the *whirlwind* (God) shall scatter them: and thou shalt rejoice in the LORD, and shalt glory in the Holy One of Israel.' Israel fans first; God's whirlwind comes second.

GLOSSARY

Israel fans first, and even that wind 'shall carry them away', but finally God's own whirlwind 'shall scatter them.' Thus in Daniel chapter two, referring to both these actions it says (vs 34–35) 'a stone was cut out without hands, which smote the image upon his feet that were of iron and clay, and brake them to pieces. Then was the iron, the clay, the brass, the silver, the gold, broken to pieces together, and became like the chaff of the summer threshingfloors; and the wind carried them away, that no place was found for them: and the stone that smote the image became a great mountain, and filled the whole earth.' It is no doubt highly significant that the United Kingdom has as a symbol the Coronation Stone, which is Jacob's pillow from Bethel, upon which each new monarch is crowned on David's throne.

The Antichrist – see Antichrist(s).

The Beast – see Beast.

The Chambers – see Chambers.

The Dragon – see Dragon.

The False prophet – see False prophet.

The Isles – see Isles.

The Islands – see Isles.

The kings of the east – see Kings of the east.

The king of the north – see King of the north.

The king of the south – see King of the south.

The Man of Sin – see Antichrist(s) and False prophet.

The Millennium – see Millennium.

The Place of Safety – see Place of safety.

The Second Coming – see Second Coming.

The Son of Perdition – see Antichrist(s) and False prophet.

The Stone Kingdom – see Stone Kingdom.

True Jew(s) – see Jew(s), True.

SUBJECT INDEX

A

Abaddon, 27, 52
Abomination of desolation, 86–7
Adam, 107–8
Africa, 2, 70
Algeria, 158
Antichrist(s), 59–60, 64, 87, 154–5, 165–6
Antipater, 119
Antitrinity, 32
Arabia, 70, 126, 168
Arabs, 7, 29, 80, 159
Armageddon, 157
Armies, angelic, 126, 133
 human, 126, 133
 of God, 126, 129
 of Satan, 133
Assyria, 109
Atomic war, 51
Australia, 8, 47, 70
Austria, 5
Awakening, the, 106

B

Babylon, 3 *et seq.*, 7, 18 *et seq.*, 33, 35 *et seq.*, 105
 economic fall of, 36
 the fall of, 19, 26
Babylon the Great, 57
Babylonian empire, 19
 system, 36 *et seq.*
Balfour Declaration, 154
Beast, 5, 7, 10, 19 *et seq.*, 33, 116 *et seq.*
 lamb-like, 7
 mark of the, 39–41
Belgium, 103, 112
Bird, evil, 10
Bird, ravenous, 8, 80

Black horse(man), 3, 35, 117
Blindness of Israel, 91 *et seq.*
Blood, plague of, 48
Body, the, 133, 137, 150
 of Moses, 136
Book of life, 38
Bottomless pit, 6, 14, 27, 52
Britain (see: Great Britain)
British Isles, the, 6 (see also, Isles, the)
 Throne, 11 (see also, Throne of David)

C

Canada, 8, 47, 70, 170
Chambers, the, 9, 15, 42, 45, 110, 121, 127
 (see also: Place(s) of safety and GLOSSARY)
 cleansing of, 79, 112
China, 8, 53, 70, 80, 120, 126, 165, 168
Christ, (see: Lord Jesus Christ)
Church, the, 35, 107
 falling away of, 88, 99
 militant, 130
 Satan among the, 41
 Satan's target, 14
 suffering of the, 41
Church, Roman, (see: Roman Church)
Com-Mark, 39
Common Market, 12, 103
 (see also: European Economic Community)
Commonwealth, 74
Communion Service, 60
Communism, -ists, 3, 31, 39 *et seq.*, 45, 70, 79
 attack in Britain, 11 *et seq.*, 100
 dictator, 26
 plot, 100

Covenant(s), Davidic (see: Davidic covenant)
  Levitical, (see: Levitical covenant)
  New, (see: New Covenant)
Cup of trembling, (see: Jerusalem)
Cush, 169
Czechoslovakia, 5

D

Davidic covenant, 65
Day of grace, 28, 38
Day of judgment, 28
Dead Sea, 53
Death, 136, 141–2
Denmark, 103, 112
Destroyer, the, 27
Devil, the, (see: Dragon, Satan and Serpent)
Dictator, 4, 26
Dragon, 6, 10 *et seq.*, 19, 46
  (see also: Satan and Serpent)

E

Eagles, 148
Earthquake, 159
East, kings of the, (see: Kings of the east)
Economics, 3, 23
Edom, 119
Egypt, 44, 109, 119, 126, 159, 168
Eire, (see: Ireland)
Elect, the, 16
Elements of Nature, 127
Elijah, 11, 67, 84, 134, 136
Empires, 3–4, 19
Ephraim, 13, 47
Esau, 119
Ethiopia, 126, 158, 169
  (see also: Cush)
Euphrates, river, 8, 53
Europe, 13, 57, 70
  armies of, 117, 121, 126
European Economic Community, 99
Exploiters, 36

F

False prophet, the, 10, 53, 58, 67, 80
  (see: GLOSSARY)
Fire, from heaven, 102
Flood, 10
Forces of nature, 43
  (see also: Elements of nature)
Forehead, 27
Four horses, 2, 116 *et seq.*
France, 5, 12, 29, 103
Frogs, 7, 53
Fullness of the Gentiles, 76

G

Gate, of enemies, 48, 49
Gentile nations, 13, 35, 43
Gentiles, 1, 21, 27, 29, 41, 90 *et seq.*
  times of the, 1, 116
Germany, 5, 12, 47, 103, 109
Gog, 10, 80, 116 *et seq.*, 161
Gospel writers, 86, 112–13
Grace, day of, 28, 38
Great Britain, 46–7, 74, 103, 169
Great tribulation, 103–4
Greece, 3, 5, 19, 102
Greek Empire, 3, 19

H

H-bombs, 102
Haifa, 160
Hammer & sickle, 128
Hell, 135
Herod, 119
High Priesthood, 163
Holland, 103, 112
Hooks in jaws, 122
Horses, four, 2, 116 *et seq.*
Hungary, 5

I

Idumean(s), 119
Image of the beast, 33
Inquisition, 4
Iran, 3, 19, 158
Iraq, 3, 19

SUBJECT INDEX

Ireland, 47, 70, 103
Ishmael, 7
Isles, the, 15, 91
Israel, defence of, 10 et seq.
  entanglement with Babylon, 21
  God's weapon(s), 43
  regathering of, 41–42
  reunion of, 70, 74
  Satan's target, 10, 14, 107–8
  separation from Babylon, 24
  the gate of their enemies, 48, 49
Israel nations, 8, 41–42, 169
Israeli state, 56, 80
Israelis, 29, 166
Italy, 3, 5, 12, 102, 103

J

Jacob's trouble, 13, 35, 98 et seq.
Japan, 56, 70, 80
Japheth, 121
Jerusalem, 1, 55, 67, 81, 84, 124, 145–6, 154, 157, 162 et seq.
  British capture of (1917), 1, 116
  cup of trembling, 66, 84, 166
  final evil ruler of, 65
Jesus Christ, (see: Lord Jesus Christ)
Jewish wealth in Palestine, 55
Jewry, (see: Jews, the)
Jews, the, 21, 36, 66–7, 81–3
  false, 80, 83
  Gentile, 67
  true, 80, 83
Jordan, river, 53
Joseph, 47
Judah, 24, 56–7, 67, 69
  nation of, 65
Judas, 28
Judgment, day of, 28

K

King of the north, 31, 63, 116 et seq., 160 (see: GLOSSARY)
King of the south, 10, 80, 161 (see: GLOSSARY
Kingdom of God, 14, 107
Kingdoms of this world, 107
Kings of the east, 8, 53
  (see: GLOSSARY)

L

Lamb, 6, 10, 54, 58
  the, 38, 59
  song of the, 92
Laser(s), 102
Laws in Israel, 74
Lebanon, 124, 160
Levi, tribe of, 66, 68, 83
Levites, 66–8
Levitical covenant, 65, 68, 81
Libya (Libians), 126, 158
Lions, young, 54
Living waters, 145
Lord Jesus Christ, 16, 89–91. 116, 126, 163
  as Judge, 68, 90, 93
  First Coming of, 1, 68
  Second Coming of, (see: Second Coming)
  temptation of, 108
  the Saviour, 68
Luxembourg, 103, 112

M

Magog, 10, 51, 120–21
Man of Sin, 57–9, 61–4, 87
  (see also: Antichrist and False prophet)
Mark, (see: Com-Mark)
Mark of the beast, 39–40
Mecca, 7, 80, 161
Mediterranean Sea, 48, 158–9
Medo-Persian Empire, 3, 19, 109
Megiddo, 160
Meshech, 80, 121
Messenger, the, 67
Michael (the Archangel), 16, 30, 114, 136, 152
Millennium, the, 135
Morocco, 158
Moses, 136
Mosque of Omar, 87, 163
Mother of harlots, 20
Mount of Olives, 87, 157
Mount of the Congregation, 11
Mount of Transfiguration, 136

N

Nations, 14, 29
   final political division of, 70
   United, (see: United Nations Organisation)
Nebuchadnezzar's dream image, 3, 18 et seq.
New birth, 114–15
New Covenant, 76, 110
New song, 92
New Zealand, 8, 47, 70, 170
Nicodemus, 115
Nile, river, 53
North Atlantic Treaty Organisation (N.A.T.O.), 13, 99, 102
North, king of the (see: King of the north)
Northern house of Israel, 46
Nuclear War, 51

O

Oil, 35, 72
Olive tree, 35
Olives, Mount of (see: Mount of Olives)
One hundred and forty-four thousand, (see: 144,000)

P

Pale horse(man), 3, 23, 117
Palestine, 8, 42, 53–8, 117, 123–4, 157
Parables, 79, 82, 100
Perdition, son of (see: GLOSSARY)
Permissive society, 13
Persia, 19, 158
Phut, 158
Place(s) of safety, 42
   (see also: Chambers and GLOSSARY)
Plague(s), 51
   Egyptian, 44–5
   last, 44 et seq.
   sores, 46
Political parties, 105
Portugal, 5, 102
Propaganda, 10
Prophecy, purpose of, 6
Prophet, false (see: False prophet) that, 65

R

Rapture of the Church, 61
Ravenous bird, 8, 80
Red horse(man), 2, 116
Red Sea deliverance, 50, 169
Redeemer, the, 17
Resurrection(s), 130–32, 135, 146 et seq.
   of the body, 133
   of the Lord, 135
Rhodesia, 70, 169
Roman Church, 5, 19–20, 32, 59, 87
Roman Empire, 4, 19
Rome, 3, 19, 109–10
Russia, 5, 19, 33, 51, 70, 79, 83, 99, 103, 117
Russian invasion of Britain, (intended), 79, 122, 157–8
Russian invasion of Palestine, 7, 123, 155 et seq., 169

S

S.E.A.T.O., 99
Saints, 38, 80, 133
Salvation, national, 114
   personal, 114–15
Satan, 7–8, 11–12, 27–9, 107 et seq., 136
   (see also: Dragon and Serpent)
   defeat of, 23, 129, 133, 149
Saudi Arabia, (see: Arabs and Arabia)
Scarlet beast, 4
Scorpion, 27, 52
Sea gate, 48
Sea trade, 37
Sealed servants of God, 40
Second Coming, the, 1, 21, 23, 58, 61–2, 85, 147–50
Serpent, 10 (see also: Dragon and Satan)
Sheol, 135
Ships of Tarshish, (see: Tarshish)
Sickle, (see: Hammer and sickle)
Solemn assembly, 165
Son of Perdition, (see: GLOSSARY)
Sores, (see: Plague(s))
Soul, 134–6
Soul sleep, 138–40
South Africa, 8, 47, 70, 170

SUBJECT INDEX

South America, 126
Spain, 5, 109
Spirit, 134
Spoil, great, 55
Stalin, 30–31
Stone Kingdom, 4, 18–19
  (see: GLOSSARY)
Suez canal, 53
Syria, 160

T

Tarshish, ships of, 54
Temple, the, 81
  rebuilding, of, 162–3
Ten Horns, 5, 57, 103
That Prophet, 65
Throne of David, 9, 11, 42, 47, 66, 129, 144 (see also: British Throne)
Time of trouble, 16
Trade recession, 37
Trade Unions, 11, 12, 100
Transfiguration, the, 136
Treaty of Rome, 21
Trees, 27
Tribe of Judah, (see: Judah)
Tribe of Levi, (see: Levi, tribe of)
Tribulation, the great, 103
Trinity, the, 32
Tubal, 80
Tunisia, 158
Turkey, 5
Turks, 1

U

Unclean spirits, 7, 53
Unions, Trade, 11, 12, 100
United Nations Organisation (U.N.O.), 99
United States of America (U.S.A.), 8, 47, 70, 94

V

Vial(s), 46, 52
Vietnam, 47, 72
Virgin daughter of Babylon, 20

W

Warsaw Pact, 99
Weapon(s), 13
  Israel, God's weapons, 44
  of God, 43–4, 127
White horse(man), 2, 116
White raiment, 144
White stone, 40
Whore, 57
Wilderness, 95–6
Wine, 35
Wine of wrath, 41
Witnesses, two, 27
Woman, 15
Wonders, 16, 33, 102

Z

Zacharias, 1

A.D. 70; 56, 155
A.D. 1917; 1, 83, 116, 119, 166
A.D. 1945; 2
A.D. 1948; 2, 56, 154, 166
A.D. 1967; 2, 154
2 Witnesses, 27
4 Beasts, 35
4 Horses, 2, 116 *et seq.*
10 Horns, 5, 57, 103
10 Toes, 103
666, 40
1,000 years, 14, 23, 41, 52
7,000 men, 15
144,000; 15–16

SCRIPTURE INDEX

Scriptures quoted or mentioned in Chapters 1–19 of this book

GENESIS

ch. 1 vs 26–28	143
ch. 9 v. 1	109
ch. 10 v. 2	121
ch. 15 v. 15	39
ch. 18 v. 14	48
ch. 22 v. 17	49
ch. 35 vs 18–19	134

EXODUS

ch. 5 vs 6–12	45
ch. 8 vs 22–23	45
ch. 12 v. 23	40
ch. 13 v. 17	50
ch. 14 v. 9	50
ch. 19 v. 6	44

NUMBERS

ch. 2 v. 32	71

DEUTERONOMY

ch. 15 vs 4–5	36
ch. 18 v. 15	65
ch. 18 vs 18–19	65

II SAMUEL

ch. 7 v. 10	157
ch. 12 vs 22–23	138

I KINGS

ch. 10 v. 22	54
ch. 12 v. 16	87
ch. 17 vs 19–22	134
ch. 22 v. 48	54

JOB

ch. 19 v. 23	131
ch. 19 vs 23–27	133
ch. 19 vs 25–27	131

PSALMS

Psalm 2 vs 1–3	8
Psalm 8 vs 4–9	143
Psalm 11 v. 6	167
Psalm 16 v. 10	131
Psalm 46 vs 1–2	93
Psalm 46 vs 1, 6–7	9
Psalm 46 v. 4	145
Psalm 46 vs 4–5	94
Psalm 46 vs 6–9	94
Psalm 46 vs 8–9	9
Psalm 46 vs 8–11	78
Psalm 46 v. 10	94
Psalm 46 vs 10–11	9
Psalm 50 vs 1–6	132, 152
Psalm 50 vs 7–8	153
Psalm 50 vs 14–15	153
Psalm 50 vs 16–21	153
Psalm 50 vs 22–23	153
Psalm 63 v. 7	169
Psalm 68 vs 18–20	136
Psalm 72 v. 8	145
Psalm 75 v 8	167
Psalm 79 v 9	13
Psalm 81 vs 13–14 & 16	73
Psalm 96 vs 1–2 & 13	92

ISAIAH

ch. 10 v. 34	124
ch. 13 vs 1–6	19
ch. 14 v. 13	11, 108
ch. 14 v. 14	108

SCRIPTURE INDEX

ISAIAH – *cont.*

ch. 14 vs 15–16	117
ch. 18 v. 1	169
ch. 18 v. 2	169
ch. 18 vs 3–6	170
ch. 18 v. 7	170
ch. 26 vs 9–12	77
ch. 26 v. 19	130, 133
ch. 26 vs 20–21	14, 24, 34
	42, 127, 131
ch. 29 v. 9	166
ch. 30 v. 15	78
ch. 33 v. 17	141
ch. 34 v. 8	105
ch. 35 v. 4	105
ch. 37 vs 29 & 33–37	122
ch. 40	67
ch. 40 v. 15	6
ch. 42 vs 1–2	89
ch. 42 vs 1–4	128
ch. 42 v. 3	90
ch. 42 v. 4	90
ch. 42 v. 5	91
ch. 42 v. 6	91
ch. 42 v. 7	92
ch. 42 v. 8	92
ch. 42 v. 9	92
ch. 42 v. 10	92
ch. 42 vs 12–14	93
ch. 42 v. 13	158
ch. 42 vs 13–15	128
ch. 42 v. 14	129
ch. 42 vs 14–15	93
ch. 42 vs 16–17	94
ch. 42 vs 18–21	95
ch. 42 v. 22	97
ch. 42 v. 24	97
ch. 43 vs 1–2	103
ch. 43 vs 1–3 & 5–7	75
ch. 43 vs 5–7	41
ch. 43 v. 6	79
ch. 43 vs 5–8	104
ch. 43 vs 22 & 24	62
ch. 46 vs 10–11	7
ch. 46 v. 11	120
ch. 47 v. 1	20
ch. 47 vs 3–4	21
ch. 47 v. 5	21
ch. 47 v. 6	21
ch. 47 vs 7–8	21
ch. 47 v. 9	23
ch. 47 v. 10	22
ch. 47 vs 12–13	22
ch. 48	56
ch. 48 vs 1–2	56
ch. 48 vs 3–5 & 8	82
ch. 48 vs 3–11	56
ch. 48 vs 8–11	57
ch. 48 vs 9–10	82
ch. 48 vs 12–22	57
ch. 48 v. 20	24
ch. 49 vs 2–3	171
ch. 51 vs 21–23	166
ch. 52 v. 11	79
ch. 52 v. 12	127
ch. 54 v. 4	22
ch. 54 v. 17	13
ch. 59 vs 9–10 & 13	16
ch. 59 v. 16	17
ch. 59 vs 19–21	17
ch. 60 v. 2	58
ch. 60 v. 9	54

JEREMIAH

ch. 3 vs 12 & 14	99
ch. 16 v. 16	75
ch 25 vs 15–16	114
ch. 25 vs 15–17	167
ch. 25 vs 16–17 & 27–28	29
ch. 25 vs 27–28	168
ch. 25 v. 29	29
ch. 30 vs 4–6	98
ch. 30 v. 7	12, 98
ch. 30 vs 12–14	101
ch. 30 vs 14–15	102
ch. 30 v. 16	105
ch. 30 v. 17	104
ch. 30 v. 18	104
ch. 30 vs 22–24	77, 104
ch. 31 vs 3 & 10–11	76
ch. 31 v. 7	165
ch. 31 v. 18	13
ch. 32	76
ch. 33 vs 17–18 & 20–22	66, 81
ch. 49 v. 16	119
ch. 50 v. 8	24
ch. 50 v. 15	105
ch. 50 vs 16 & 22–23	128
ch. 50 vs 24–25	125, 128
ch. 51 v. 5	24

SCRIPTURE INDEX

JEREMIAH – cont.
ch. 51 v. 6	24
ch. 51 vs 19–20	44
ch. 51 v. 20	127

EZEKIEL
ch. 9 vs 3–6	39
ch. 20 vs 34–35	96
ch. 23 vs 2 & 4	167
ch. 23 vs 32–33	167
ch. 34 v. 25	96
ch. 37 vs 16 & 19	47
ch. 37 vs 19–22	73
ch. 38	171
ch. 38 vs 1–2	120, 121
ch. 38 vs 3–4	46, 121
ch. 38 v. 5	158
ch. 38 v. 8	157
ch. 38 vs 9–10	123
ch. 38 vs 9–12	156
ch. 38 v. 12	123
ch. 38 v. 13	54
ch. 38 vs 15–16	157
ch. 38 vs 16–17	124
ch. 39 vs 1–2	121
ch. 39 v. 2	123
ch. 39 vs 6–7	51
ch. 47 vs 1–12	145

DANIEL
ch. 2	33, 57
ch. 2 vs 31–45	18
ch. 2 v. 35	4
ch. 5 v. 19	26
ch. 7 vs 13–14	110
ch. 10 vs 12–21	152
ch. 11	33
ch. 11 vs 30–45	118
ch. 11 vs 32–35	140
ch. 11 v. 36	31, 63, 119
ch. 11 v. 37	31
ch. 11 v. 38	32
ch. 11 v. 39	32
ch. 11 v. 40	159
ch. 11 v. 42	119
ch. 11 vs 42–43	159
ch. 11 v. 43	120
ch. 11 v. 44	161
ch. 11 vs 44–45	189 120
ch. 11 v. 45	87
ch. 12 v. 1	16, 30 114, 152
ch. 12 v. 13	130

HOSEA
ch. 2 vs 13–14	95

JOEL
ch. 2 vs 15–18	165

AMOS
ch. 9 v. 9	79

OBADIAH
vs 1–6	83
v. 4	118

MICAH
ch. 5 vs 3–5	74
ch. 6 vs 1–2	70
ch. 6 v. 3	62, 71
ch. 6 vs 4–5	71
ch. 6 vs 6–7	72
ch. 6 v. 8	72

HABAKKUK
ch. 2 vs 4–5	30
ch. 2 vs 5, 9 & 16	118
ch. 2 v. 14	30
ch. 2 vs 14 & 20	118
ch. 2 v. 18	118
ch. 2 v. 19	118

ZEPHANIAH
ch. 1 vs 4, 13–14	85
ch. 1 v. 11	2
ch. 1 vs 12–13	156
ch. 1 vs. 14–18	55, 155

ZEPHANIAH – *cont.*

ch. 1 v. 18	124
ch. 3 v. 8	168
ch. 3 v. 10	171

ZECHARIAH

ch. 9 v. 13	2
ch. 12 vs 2–3	166
ch. 12 vs 2 & 5	66
ch. 12 v. 12	84
ch. 14 vs 1–2	55
ch. 14 v. 2	120, 157
ch. 14 v. 14	55, 85
	124, 155

MALACHI

ch. 2 vs 1–2 & 4–5	68
ch. 2 vs 8 & 10	68
ch. 3 v. 1	67, 83, 84, 163
ch. 3 v. 2	67
ch. 3 vs 2–4	68
ch. 3 vs 2–5	84
ch. 4 vs 4–6	91
ch. 4 v. 5	67
ch. 4 vs 5–6	11, 84

MATTHEW

ch. 8 v. 29	111
ch. 10 v. 5	89
ch. 10 v. 28	134
ch. 13 vs 10–11 & 13–15	82
ch. 13 v. 24	101
ch. 13 v. 25	101
ch. 15 v. 24	89
ch. 21 v. 43	83
ch. 23 v. 35	130
ch. 24 vs 15–16	85
ch. 24 v. 21	103
ch. 24 vs 22–24	16
ch. 24 vs 27–28	148
ch. 24 vs 29–31	148
ch. 24 v. 31	151
ch. 27 v. 51	164
ch. 27 vs 52–53	137
ch. 28 v. 20	89

MARK

ch. 13 v. 14	86
ch. 15 vs 11	69

LUKE

ch. 4 vs 5–7	108
ch. 8 v. 28	111
ch. 17 v. 22	1
ch. 21 v. 24	1, 116
ch. 22 v. 3	127
ch. 23 v. 23	69

JOHN

ch. 1 vs 1 & 14	86
ch. 3 v. 7	115
ch. 4 vs 19–23	164
ch. 5 vs 25 & 28–29	137
ch. 7 v. 46	115
ch. 7 v. 51	115
ch. 10 vs 30–33	63
ch. 11 vs 23–27	146
ch. 12 vs 47–48	90
ch. 14 vs 2–3	137
ch. 14 v. 3	141
ch. 17 v. 12	88
ch. 19 v. 6	69

ACTS

ch. 2 vs 26–27	135
ch. 7 v. 37	65
ch. 17 v. 30	96

ROMANS

ch. 3 vs 1–2	83
ch. 8 v. 1	132
ch. 11 vs 2–4	15
ch. 11 v. 17	35
ch. 11 v. 25	2, 76
ch. 11 vs 25–26	96
ch. 11 vs 25–27	91
ch. 11 v. 26	76
ch. 12 vs 17–21	49
ch. 12 v. 19	37

SCRIPTURE INDEX

I CORINTHIANS

ch. 11 vs 25–26	60
ch. 15 vs 51–52	150, 151
ch. 15 vs 53–57	151

II CORINTHIANS

ch. 5 vs 1–8	138
ch. 11 vs 12–15	12

EPHESIANS

ch. 2 vs 1–2	148
ch. 2 v. 2	28

PHILIPPIANS

ch. 1 vs 21–24	138

I THESSALONIANS

ch. 4 vs 13–14	149
ch. 4 vs 15–17	149
ch. 4 v. 16	151

II THESSALONIANS

ch. 1 vs 7–8	133
ch. 1 vs 7–12	61
ch. 2 vs 1–2	61
ch. 2 v. 3	57, 62, 87
ch. 2 vs 3–4	63, 88, 164
ch. 2 vs 4–8	64
ch. 2 v. 8	88
ch. 2 vs 9–10	64
ch. 2 vs 11–12	64
ch. 3 v. 10	36

HEBREWS

ch 2 vs 8–9	143
ch. 2 v. 14	23, 136
ch. 8 vs 10–12	76
ch. 10 vs 30–31	50

JAMES

ch. 5 v. 1	36

I PETER

ch. 1 v. 10	153
ch. 2 v. 9	127
ch. 3 vs 18–19	137
ch. 5 v. 8	11

II PETER

ch. 3 vs 10 & 13	52

I JOHN

ch. 2 v. 18	59
ch. 2 vs 18 & 21–23	59

II JOHN

v. 7	59

JUDE

v. 9	136

REVELATION

ch. 3 vs 12	40
ch. 5 v. 1	139
ch. 5 vs 2–3	139
ch. 5 vs 5–7	139
ch. 5 vs 5–10	144
ch. 5 vs 9–10	139
ch. 5 v. 14	35
ch. 6 v. 2	2
ch. 6 v. 4	2
ch. 6 vs 5–6	35
ch. 6 vs 7–8	23, 117
ch. 6 vs 9–11	140
ch. 6 vs 10–11	58
ch. 6 v. 11	140
ch. 6 vs 12–17	148
ch. 7 vs 1–4	15
ch. 7 vs 2–3	40
ch. 7 vs 9–10	140
ch. 7 vs 9–10 & 13–17	145
ch. 7 vs 13–15	141
ch. 8 vs 8–9	48
ch. 8 vs 10–11	48

REVELATION – *cont.*

ch. 9	113	ch. 16 v. 2	123
ch. 9 vs 1–2	27	ch. 16 v. 3	48
ch. 9 v. 4	27	ch. 16 v. 4	49
ch. 9 v. 6	27	ch. 16 vs 5–7	49
ch. 9 v. 11	27	ch. 16 vs 8–9	51
ch. 9 vs 13–14	49	ch. 16 vs 10–11	52
ch. 11 v. 15	23, 107, 111	ch. 16 v. 12	8, 53
ch. 11 vs 15–18	8	ch. 16 vs 13–14	7, 53, 116
ch. 11 v. 18	111	ch. 16 v. 14	58
ch. 12 vs 7–8	152	ch. 17 vs 1–5	20
ch. 12 vs 7–10	114	ch. 17 vs 3–7	4
ch. 12 v. 12	10	ch. 17 v. 5	57
ch. 12 v. 14	79	ch. 17 vs 9–10	4
ch. 12 v. 15–16	10	ch. 17 v. 12	159
ch. 12 vs 16–17	15	ch. 17 vs 12–13	5
ch. 12 v. 17	46, 78, 121, 158	ch. 17 vs 13–14	122
ch. 13	87	ch. 17 vs 15–16 & 18	5
ch. 13 vs 3–4	5	ch. 17 v. 16	57
ch. 13 vs 4–6	33	ch. 18 v. 2	26, 27
ch. 13 vs 7–8	38	ch. 18 vs 1–2	114
ch. 13 v. 11	6, 54, 58	ch. 18 vs 1–4	25
ch. 13 vs 11–18	118	ch. 18 vs 4–5	42
ch. 13 vs 12–14	33	ch. 18 vs 7–8	25
ch. 13 v. 13	102	ch. 18 vs 10–11	37
ch. 13 v. 15	33	ch. 18 vs 14–15	37
ch. 13 v. 16	39	ch. 18 vs 17–19	37
ch. 13 v. 17	38	ch. 18 vs 20–21 & 24	37
ch. 14 v. 8	25	ch. 20 vs 1–2	6
ch. 14 vs 9–10	38, 41	ch. 20 vs 1–6	130
ch. 14 vs 12–13	147	ch. 20 v. 4	41
ch. 14 v. 14	151	ch. 20 vs 4–6	135
ch. 14 vs 14–16	147	ch. 20 vs 6 & 11–15	132
ch. 16	45, 58	ch. 21 vs 1–4	146
ch. 16 vs 1–2	46	ch. 22 vs 1–2	146
		ch. 22 vs 10–11	39